This book is dedicated to my three sons:
Brock, Zach, and Caleb.
It has been awesome to be your dad. Watching
you make decisions better than I did at your age
is one of the sweetest experiences of my life.
"I have no greater joy than to hear that my
children are walking in the truth."

—3 John 14

Contents

Acknowledgments

The writing of this book has been a 30-year journey that started with a conversation with my father. Dad, you had no idea you would create the hunger in me that you did to pursue the process of decision-making, but I am thankful for your example. You always did what you loved in your career, which gave me confidence I could do the same.

My brother helped fuel the fire. Jim, the way you focused on prayerful decisions when you entered college inspired me to believe that we could live excellent lives. Your example has proved invaluable to me.

I am confident I would have made smaller decisions had I not married the woman of my dreams. Pam, you are the most courageous woman I have ever met, and I am forever grateful that you challenged me to live a bigger life while you cheered me on with relentless encouragement. You have proven to be a super incredible helpmate.

I would also like to say thank you to Bob Hawkins and the entire staff at Harvest House Publishers. Thanks for taking a chance on a young, idealistic couple and giving us an opportunity to tell our story. You did us a big favor when you assigned Rod Morris to be our editor. Rod, thanks for using your talents to make the message clearer and easier to read. Your command of the language, breadth of knowledge, and excellence in editing has been a huge gift. For your sake, I hope Kansas State makes the Final Four soon.

Finally, I want to say thank you to my Savior, Jesus Christ. You found me when I was 16 in the padded seat of a movie theatre and have taken me on a thrill ride ever since. It is humbly exhilarating to be in this remarkably unequal partnership.

Introduction

We make our choices and our choices make us.

I remember when my journey into trying to figure out how to make good decisions began. It was the summer between my senior year in high school and my freshman year in college. I was looking ahead to my university education, and I wanted to pursue a degree that would set me up for success. So I went to my dad for advice because he loved his career.

My dad worked in the aerospace industry designing rocket engines. His job was to design the process for igniting, accelerating, and shutting down engines that would propel astronauts, scientists, and satellites into space. I admired his optimism and dedication to his career, even though the program had many critics.

One of the early pioneers of rocket technology was Robert Goddard. On March 16, 1926, he drove to his aunt Effie's farm to test fire his spindly, 10-foot tall liquid fuel rocket named Nell. The rocket leaped into the air, climbed to a height of 41 feet, then slammed into a frozen cabbage patch. The flight lasted just 2.5 seconds, but it was 2.5 seconds longer than any liquid-fueled rocket had flown before. He was thrilled and recognized the breakthrough for what it was.

Goddard kept his research and testing under wraps for the next three years, but rockets are hard to hide. In 1929 one of his launches led to the arrival of the police, which led to the presence of the press. The headline in the local press the next day read, "MOON ROCKET MISSES TARGET BY 238,799½ MILES."[1] Despite the criticism, Goddard pressed on, and history bears the mark of his vision.

My dad had this same optimism. He could often be heard to say,

"I can't believe they pay me to do this job." I concluded that if anyone knew how to choose a career, it would be my dad.

"Dad, can I ask you a question?"

"Sure, Bill, what is it?"

"How do you figure out what you should do for a career? How does a young man my age decide on a college degree?"

I was anticipating that I would have the most profound conversation of my life with my dad. Instead, he said, "Well, Bill, I am not good at talking about things like this, but I will support whatever you choose."

I was still confident that my dad knew how I could choose a career I would love. He just didn't know how to communicate the process that would lead me there. I didn't realize it at the time, but my desire to learn how good decisions are made began that day. I wanted to be able to communicate with others what I saw my dad model for me.

Since that day, I have been intently watching men make decisions. Some of these decisions have led to growing businesses, strong families, and solid lives. Other decisions have been self-destructive. The majority of the decisions, however, have been attempts to stay ahead of the challenges of life. Sometimes these decisions work out well and sometimes they fall short. It is often a mystery why some decisions work out while others fail to deliver the anticipated results.

I set out to discover how I could make deliberate, forward thinking, productive decisions in my life. What I have learned, I will share with you in the chapters that follow. As you read, I trust you will grow in your understanding of how to benefit from healthy decision-making.

It's Your Turn

In the space below or on a separate sheet of paper, describe when your journey into decision-making began. What conversations, situations, or challenges did you face that helped create a need to know how to make better decisions?

Chapter 1

Decide to Be Decisive

*"Learn as if you were to live forever; live
as if you were to die tomorrow."*

—John Wooden[1]

I have never met a man who said he wants to make poor decisions. The men I have met love their families and are genuinely looking to be successful in life. We all know, however, that men with good intentions sometimes make bad decisions because our intentions don't determine the quality of our decisions. There is a significant difference between the men who make good decisions and those who complicate their lives with either indecisiveness or decisions that defy the way life was meant to be.

The Benefits of Good Decisions

Numerous benefits develop in a man's life when he decides to be decisive. First and foremost, *he has more energy for the pursuits he cares about.* This happens because our emotions follow our decisions. This is how we steer our emotions so they do not run their own path.

Men are often thought of as nonemotional or less emotional than women, but this is not true. We are just different emotionally. Just watch a man at a sporting event. When things go well, he yells and pumps his fist in the air. When things are not going well, he gets angry and often voices his displeasure. Watch another man working on a project. He gets excited when things work well, and he often gets angry when things won't cooperate.

I recently visited a friend who owns a large area of grass he likes to mow himself. To tackle the job, he purchased a "Bad Boy" lawnmower.

It came complete with a Caterpillar diesel motor and has a zero degree turn radius. He had that "this is really manly" look on his face as he said to me, "This mower's motto is, 'We cut with attitude,' and I can mow grass at 15 miles per hour with this Bad Boy." Just to prove his point, he fired up the mower, proceeded to burn out the tires, and turned circles in his shed. It was an impressive machine that elicited an emotional and manly response.

I am convinced that Karl is free to be enthused and full of energy because he is an excellent decision-maker. He has, for years, channeled his energy into a productive, balanced, and inspiring life.

Decisions also make us more efficient. Some people follow the mistaken notion that says, "We never have time to do a thing right, but we always have time to do it over." It is just more efficient to choose well from the outset.

Decisions simplify our lives. Our lives are an interconnected web of relationships. Decisions that are compatible with the way God designed life make relationships work better, create fewer negative consequences, and minimize the situations we need to clean up after the fact. As a result, good decisions develop a life where relationships need less maintenance and recovery from complicated interactions.

Healthy decisions raise your confidence level. Any time you are convinced that you are doing what you were designed to do, your focus, dedication, and motivation are high. There is simply no hesitation. You do what needs to be done. You say what needs to be said. You research what you do not know, and you get into action. There is no second guessing, no what-ifs, and no overanalysis.

When it comes to decisions, there are three categories of men:

- Those who operate in HD (Healthy Decisions). These men mostly make decisions that are healthy and lead to productive, relationally satisfying outcomes.

- Those who operate in UD (Unhealthy Decisions). The decisions these men make are mostly unhealthy and short-sighted. They often find themselves in complicated situations and awkward relationships.

- Those who operate in ND (Nondecisions). These men allow others to make decisions for them or they avoid making choices and let life turn out however it wants to. This approach leads to codependent relationships, underachieving, emotional turmoil, missed opportunities, and immature interactions.

Men fall into several traps that slow the process of personal growth and keep them from healthy decisions:

- They let others make decisions for them that they should be making for themselves.
- They blame poor decisions on others.
- They decide they don't need to make changes because "that's the way they've always been."
- They make excuses for not making decisions.
- They refuse to set priorities that could guide their decisions.
- They are too lazy to make the effort it takes.
- They give in to peer pressure rather than deciding what is best.
- They are not honest about the changes they know deep down need to be made.

Which of these traps are you most susceptible to?

The journey of our lives is filled with decisions. Every day we must make decisions about what food we will eat, how we will spend our time, and who we will spend that time with. Most of these decisions are minor in nature, but they come in rapid fashion. One result of the information age is a never-ending stream of data that requires almost constant decision-making.

Strategic decision-making makes life more efficient and gives momentum to your pursuit of God's will. Insufficient decision-making complicates your life and robs you of energy and opportunities. Notice the priority of decision-making in Deuteronomy 30:19-20:

> This day I call heaven and earth as witnesses against you that
> I have set before you life and death, blessings and curses.
> *Now choose life*, so that you and your children may live and
> that you may love the LORD your God, listen to his voice,
> and hold fast to him. For the LORD is your life, and he will
> give you many years in the land he swore to give to your
> fathers, Abraham, Isaac and Jacob.

God challenged His people to pay attention and make decisions that protect and enhance our lives. He knows that life is made up of one vital decision after another. Every day you are faced with life and death decisions, and you must be determined to choose well if you are to avoid situations that can destroy everything you have worked to establish.

I got a stark reminder of this truth in a phone call from my son Zachery.

"Dad, I am so mad right now."

"Really, what's up?"

"I just got in an accident."

"Oh man, are you all right?"

"Yeah, but I am really mad."

"Why are you so mad?"

"Because I never saw him coming. I had the green light and he totally ran the red light."

It turned out it wasn't quite as simple as he described to me. He was turning left at one of those intersections that has a combination traffic signal. At the beginning of the cycle, there is a left arrow that directs people in the turn lane to proceed. It then turns to a green light with a reminder, "left turn yield to traffic on green light." Well, the light had changed but Zach didn't notice. At the same time, the other driver assumed everything was clear so he never slowed down as he entered the intersection. The pictures were sickening. My son was driving a full-sized Dodge Ram pickup. The other vehicle was a Jeep Grand Cherokee. The front of the Jeep plowed into the passenger side fender of the Dodge. The front wheel ended up where the engine should be. The engine was pointing 45 degrees in the wrong direction and the fender was totally collapsed. The bumper was catapulted onto the sidewalk, and the cab of the truck was barely recognizable.

My son's massive, tough, seemingly indestructible truck was completely totaled and reduced to a pile of pathetic scrap metal and spare parts. All because two men were not alert for a moment in time. It didn't take long. It didn't involve any advanced planning. But it could have changed my son's life for the rest of his days—or ended his life because it was a life-and-death decision. He chose poorly, but, fortunately for him, the only thing that was broken up was his truck.

The next time you are unexpectedly faced with a life-and-death decision, what will you choose?

The most common method for making decisions is to do so by instinct. You are faced with a decision. Your instincts kick into gear based upon your life experience and your emotional programming. A decision "occurs" to you that feels right. In the absence of any other decisions that seem better, you commit to this course of action.

Frank Crane comments on the drawbacks of this accidental approach to decision-making: "Most of the things we decide are not what we know to be the best. We say yes, merely because we are driven into a corner and must say something."[2] But Sigmund Freud actually encouraged this type of decision-making:

> When making a decision of minor importance, I have always found it advantageous to consider all the pros and cons. In vital matters, however, such as the choice of a mate or a profession, the decision should come from the unconscious, from somewhere within ourselves. In the important decisions of personal life, we should be governed, I think, by the deep inner needs of our nature.[3]

If the emotional programming of your life is healthy, these natural decisions can be strong and effective. If, however, the emotional programming is flawed or underdeveloped, these natural decisions are generally shortsighted and lead to complicated results.

You Can Decide to Be Different

This was one the first things I encountered in my own journey. My home was characterized by a lot of fear. My mom was afraid of people, bugs, driving, and anything that allowed others to be involved in our lives. In her attempts to control her life, she would get angry, depressed, or long-winded. She could lecture for hours, erupt in anger, or hide for days.

As the youngest in my family, I watched my older brother and sister fight with my mom. I concluded that approach didn't work, so I went the other direction and grew numb. I wasn't aware of it when I was growing up, but as an adult, I began to realize that I was programmed to grow numb under stress and to grow stubborn around anyone who doesn't make sense to me. Since most decisions involve some level of stress, and often involve people who share differing opinions, this was a problem.

Early in my adult years, I discovered that helping people was what I liked most, but I was trained to isolate myself and not to trust people. I was skilled as a kid at spending long periods of time by myself avoiding the stress of my mom's fear. As a result, I had an ongoing argument within myself. My desire would say, *Invite people over. Have dinner together. Watch sporting events together. Have a Bible study in your home.* My instincts would push back, *You don't know what they might do. You don't know if you can really trust them. They might find out too much about your life and use it against you.*

As a result, I noticed a big gap between what I wanted to do and what I was actually doing. It even showed up in the car I drove. I wanted to drive a cool car. I dreamed of a car with a powerful engine, awesome styling, and a great paint job. Instead, I drove a green 1972 Chevrolet Vega with a blue back door. It had a blue door because I broke the back window carrying a woodshop project, and it was cheaper to get a door at the junkyard than to replace the window. Besides, I had plans to paint the car.

I had read the reports about the aluminum block that tended to crack when it overheated, but I was convinced it would not happen to me. I read books about how to "hot rod" your Vega. I read articles about how to put a V-8 motor in this pocket rocket, and I dreamed of having a car that would be the envy of my friends. I had plans, but they never turned into decisions. So I just kept driving my Vega. All my friends noticed, but not for the reasons I was hoping.

We, however, are not required to make decisions by instinct. We have been equipped with the ability to discern a wise course of action in each decision of our lives. We have been given the mind of Christ (1 Corinthians 2:16), and we can utilize that ability to make effective decisions. As WWII hero William Foster says, "Quality is never an accident; it is always the result of high intention, sincere effort, intelligent direction and skillful execution; it represents the wise choice of many alternatives."[4]

Go Big

Healthy decisions cause growth in our lives. With each passing year, we are faced with challenges, opportunities, and responsibilities that seemingly are bigger and more demanding than the year before. Healthy decisions move us forward step-by-step so that each year we are prepared for what comes our way. The real complications in life come when our maturity does not match our challenges.

I used to think that some people were born with the ability to recognize and pursue healthy decisions while others were doomed to miss strategic decisions or make shortsighted choices. If that were the case, I was sure I had been left out of the group that was born to be strategic. I have since discovered that anytime we are faced with a decision, we can perform a number of tests that give guidance, clarity, and confidence to the process.

Decision-making Skill 1: The Obvious Test

When you are faced with a decision, it's helpful to determine if this is a simple decision or a more complicated choice. Before you put a lot of effort into any decision, ask yourself, "Is this decision so obvious that I am wasting time thinking about it?" The reason these decisions are obvious is that God has already clearly spoken to these areas of life or they are generally accepted as the best practices. If you put too much into these decisions, you get needlessly sidetracked and train yourself to stall when you ought to push forward. Consider these obvious decisions based on the best practices in life:

- Brush your teeth every day.
- Dress appropriately for work.

- If a police car pulls up behind you and turns its lights on, pull over.
- Get a good night's sleep regularly.
- If a friend of yours is in the hospital, go visit him.
- If a friend or family member gives you a gift, say, "Thank you."

Here are some of the most obvious decisions we face as men that have been clearly directed by the one who made us:

- Input God's Word into your mind in some way every day (Romans 12:2; Psalm 1:1-3).
- Choose what is good over what is evil (Romans 12:9).
- When faced with sexual temptation, run away (1 Thessalonians 4:3-8). Don't pray about it or investigate it, run away.
- When you want to worry, pray more intensely (Philippians 4:6-7).
- In the midst of every situation, find a way to give thanks (1 Thessalonians 5:16-18).
- Confess sin as soon as you are aware of it (1 John 1:9). Don't explain it or justify it, confess it.
- Choose your friends wisely (1 Corinthians 15:33).
- If a friend asks you to lie for him, just say no (Colossians 3:9-10).

When you train yourself to do the obvious, you develop habits in your life that become automatic. These habits make your life more efficient as they conserve your energy for more complex choices. They also raise your confidence level as success in simple tasks builds a track record of encouragement for the decisions that are not as obvious.

It's amazing to watch how this test affects men's lives. Terrance has a remarkable amount of unrealized potential because he refuses to follow this test. He is gifted in mechanical abilities and is one of the most likeable men I have ever known. People just love to be around him because his personality puts them at ease and they are fascinated by his knowledge of how things work. He simply refuses to stay consistent with the obvious choices in his life.

Terrance often gets caught up in projects and arrives home much later than he was expected. His wife would be okay with it if he would call home and let her know, but he never calls. He promises to attend his kids' activities, but then gets carried away with one of his ventures and arrives just as the activity is ending. He has experimented with illegal stimulants, which severely complicate his most important relationships. His wife doesn't trust him when it comes time to make important decisions. They discuss them at length, his suggestions are often ignored, and he has to spend an enormous amount of energy to convince her that his ideas are valid. He often just lets her decide because it is exhausting to negotiate with her.

Tom, on the other hand, has the habits of his life dialed in. He runs four or five times per week. He has a scheduled date with his wife every week. He wakes up early enough to spend 10 to 15 minutes with Jesus, reading his Bible and praying, before going to work. He has simply trained himself to do the obvious things as soon as he is aware of them. When Tom and I talk, we explore subjects such as, "How do we impact our generation to live better lives? How can we help our kids be the best they can be? How do we help our wives through the current transition in their lives?"

Terrance and I have conversations about how to survive in a changing world; Tom and I have conversations about how to change the world.

Make the obvious decision when it is obvious.

A party of suppliers was being given a tour of a mental hospital. One of the visitors had made some insulting remarks about the patients. After the tour the visitors were introduced to various staff members in the canteen. The rude visitor chatted with one of the security staff, Bill, a kindly and wise ex-policeman.

"Are they all raving loonies in here then?" said the rude man.

"Only the ones who fail the test," said Bill.

"What's the test?"

"Well, we show them a bath full of water, a bucket, a jug, and an egg-cup, and we ask them what's the quickest way to empty the bath."

"Oh I see, simple—the normal ones know it's the bucket, right?"

"No actually," said Bill, "the normal ones say pull out the plug. Should I check when there's a bed free for you?"[5]

Decision-making Skill 2: The Wisdom Test

In the space below, write down your thoughts about this question, "What is the difference between being smart and being wise?"

Not all decisions are obvious. Most of the decisions we must make require some level of discussion, deliberation, and discernment. This is why the Bible puts such a high value on wisdom, which is the ability to apply what is true to the situations of our lives in a skillful and beneficial way.

In this information age we live in, most people are not even aware of the vast amounts of information they casually discuss every day. For instance, I was talking with my youngest son the other day about a new video game he had rented. In the conversation, he referred to medieval knights and the commercial practices of medieval street vendors. He talked about swords, scabbards, spears and how they compare with ninja swords, M-16s, and incendiary explosive devices (IEDs). He also commented on computer graphics, CPU processing speed, and the meaning of the Eden treasures that were part of the pursuit in his game. He talked about all this so casually that he never realized how much more he knows at his age than any generation before him.

Knowledge, however, is much different than wisdom. My son still has trouble monitoring his schedule, managing his bank account, and trying to decide what college to attend. He often gets distracted by pursuits he loves at the expense of priorities that make his life more effective. He is intelligent, but he is still developing wisdom that matches his intelligence.

The path for developing wisdom is decorated with questions. Wise people ask questions with a sincere desire to find answers they can apply to real life. They know they will not get all their questions answered, and they are aware that their questions will change as they gain new insight and adjust to the truth they have applied to life. James 1:5 challenges all of us, "If any of you lacks wisdom, he should ask God, who gives generously to all without finding fault, and it will be given to him." The day you stop asking is the day you stop growing in wisdom.

Jesus asked His followers questions to encourage the development of wisdom. He was interested in guiding them into a deeper understanding of who He was, so He asked, "Who do people say that the Son of Man is?" After they answered, He asked, "But what about you? Who do you say I am?" (Matthew 16:13-16). He wanted them to make the issue personal so they would make a decision.

When Jesus encountered two blind men in Matthew 20, He asked them, "What do you want me to do for you?" He had the power to heal them, and He knew He would grant them their miracle, but He wanted them to make a decision. He knew that a life with sight would require them to be more responsible than when they were blind, so He wanted them to be fully invested in the new lifestyle that would be theirs.

I would never say there is only one reason Jesus asked questions of those in His world, but one of the reasons was certainly to help them develop wisdom so they could apply truth to their lives.

You can apply the Wisdom Test, therefore, by asking a set of questions when you're faced with a decision. These questions help you apply wisdom to the situation, so if you answer yes to all of them, it's clear that your decision is based on wisdom and you probably ought to proceed. If you answer no to all or most of them, you have more rigorous work to do to figure out the best course of action. The goal is to put in the least amount of effort to arrive at an effective decision. The Wisdom Test will help you conserve energy on decisions that you already possess the wisdom to make.

If the Obvious Test does not make your decision clear, ask the following questions:

- Does this decision line up with my convictions?
- Will the people I respect most agree with this decision? Have I asked them?
- Is this decision based on healthy boundaries that will produce self-respect?
- Will this decision cause personal growth in my life?
- Would I encourage my best friends to make this same decision?

Decision-making Skill 3: The Priority Test

Some decisions in life require more effort to figure out. You've gone through the Obvious Test and the Wisdom Test, but you still need more evidence that you are making the best decision. This happens when:

- The Bible doesn't specifically address the decision that is before you.
- You have many options to choose from.
- Your two best options are both attractive to you.
- The decision will impact your life for a long time to come.
- People you respect have differing opinions on how you should decide.

When this occurs, there are some simple and practical steps you can take.

Step 1: Write out your decision in a positive way. In other words, describe what you will do if you say yes to this decision. For instance, "I am considering moving my family to Colorado to begin working for a company there that would result in a pay increase." Because a description such as this encourages you to think about momentum in your life, it is better than saying, "I am considering turning down the job offer in Colorado." Whichever way you go with a decision like this, define the direction you will take if you say yes to the decision. Take full ownership of your choice and put your heart into it. You want to leave no room for negative thinking.

Step 2: Make a pro/con list. Create two columns on a sheet of paper. On one side write down the reasons why you *ought* to take this course of action. On the other side write down the reasons why this course of action is *not* a good idea.

Step 3: Prioritize the reasons. In both columns prioritize the reasons you have listed. The Bible clearly teaches that priorities lead to progress. Psalm 90:12 challenges us, "Teach us to number our days aright, that we may gain a heart of wisdom." As you prioritize your thinking, wise decisions make themselves known.

I prefer to use an ABC system to prioritize my lists. This means I assign an A to the vital reasons I identify in my list. The supportive reasons get a B. I reserve a C for the reasons I came up with because I'm creative and can come up with ideas that don't really affect the decision. Some people like to rank the reasons by importance (1, 2, 3…), so choose the scheme you are most comfortable with. For the rest of our discussion, I will assume you are using an ABC system.

Step 4: Compare the high-priority reasons from both lists. Evaluate the A reasons for saying yes with the A reasons for choosing no. If it is a tie, then move to the B reasons to see if the decision becomes clear. Don't be fooled by quantity. It is quite possible that one list will have more reasons than the other, but this is inconsequential. Quantity is no substitute for quality, and decisions such as this require high-quality conclusions. Many people will automatically choose the list that has the largest number of reasons, which creates an accidental environment for success. The list with the most reasons might be the best choice, but it might not. The way to build clarity is to deliberately prioritize the evidence and discipline yourself to focus on the A reasons.

My decision to become a senior pastor in San Diego County was one of the most interesting chapters in my life. I was 29 and idealistic. I wanted nothing more than to fulfill God's will for my life. I was willing to go anywhere and serve in any capacity to follow God's lead. I had a productive interview with one of the members of the church and decided to accept an invitation to preach at one of their services. I went with great anticipation. The service went well, so the decision-making process began. It was the first time I discovered the power of priorities in figuring out a strategic course of action.

I made a list of all the reasons I should say no to this opportunity. The list included:

- The building was poorly designed. It had been added onto twice, and a beam ran three-fourths the length of the building, bisecting the auditorium with two-thirds of the space on one side of the beam and one-third of the space on the other side. For someone who started out in college as an architecture major, this could be a constant source of irritation.

- The ceiling of the auditorium was so low that I could hit the ceiling from the platform. If I were going to preach in this facility, I would have to behave because I could easily hurt my hand if I got too enthusiastic.

- The door from the auditorium to the office was in the middle of the stage. Part of the stage actually had to be removed every Sunday night to open this door.

- The church didn't seem to be relevant to San Diego County. It had the feel of a country church in Kansas rather than a Southern California church. This included everything from the music to the style of dress to the way the landscape was designed and maintained.

- The leadership of the church was immature. One man was influential but not savvy. He was brash, unsophisticated, and opinionated. People loved him and feared him, and it was clear that everything would need his approval.

- We would be taking a pay cut to work there. I was a youth pastor at a large church with a healthy salary and benefit package. This church was smaller than the other church's youth group, and they would not be able to match the salary I had enjoyed.

- It would be harder to own a home in this community because houses cost more and I would be making less.

- The congregation was relatively uneducated. Less than half the people had college degrees, and I had recently earned my master's degree.

- The church was 25 years old and had never grown larger than 200 attendees. I think a church of 200 is a success, but the potential of a church in this area was much larger. I wasn't sure of the specific factors, but something was holding this church back.

There were only a few reasons for even considering this opportunity:

- San Diego County is a nice place to live.
- The church had a lot of potential.
- I had a strong sense that God was calling me and my family to this church.

I had a lot more reasons for saying no to this church than saying yes. I even liked the reasons for declining the invitation better than the reasons for accepting it. Had I based this decision on the number of reasons, I would never have moved to San Diego. Before I made this decision, I prioritized each of the reasons, assigning each one an A, B, or C.

I reached the conclusion that every reason on the "don't take this opportunity" list was a B priority. Two of the reasons on the "take this opportunity" list were also Bs, but the notion that God was calling us proved to be an A priority that overshadowed everything else.

Like other life decisions, I went into this opportunity with many questions. Could I overcome the obstacles this church presented? Could I help this church reach its potential? Did this group of people even want to reach their potential? Could my family handle this challenge? Would this church ever prosper enough to pay a salary that would allow us to purchase a house?

Of course, these questions did not get answered ahead of time. I had to calculate the risk and step out in faith and wait to see how it all worked out. Looking back, following the priorities was a smart move.

The church struggled along for years but eventually grew to be the largest in our community. The real accomplishment, however, was the number of ministries that were launched from that one church. Pam and I started our writing and conference ministry while we served there. A drama ministry was birthed from a talented pool of performers. A nationally recognized cameraman and a TV producer discovered their talents and the courage to pursue their dreams in this congregation. Several people joined writers' groups and have published books, magazine articles, and curricula. Many went to the mission field. That church became a vibrant hub of creativity, accountability, and courageous pursuits.

It's Your Turn

What decision do you currently face that needs the Priority Test? Describe the decision in positive terms in the space below. Then on a separate sheet of paper work through the Priority Test.

When Life Is Truly Different

The vast majority of decisions in your life can be figured out using the Obvious Test, the Wisdom Test, and the Priority Test. Every once in a while, though, you will encounter decisions that are elusive. This happens when choices present themselves that are truly *different* from decisions you have encountered in the past. You are not sure how to get started because you are into new territory with new implications. You have little life experience to draw on, no track record to look back on. In order to tackle these decisions, you need to open yourself up to new possibilities.

Decision-making Skill 4: The Brainstorm Test

This test can be strenuous so you don't want to rely on it often, but there are times when it is necessary to answer the question, "Have I considered every possible solution I can imagine?" One of our great privileges in life is to exercise our creativity. The creativity to identify and explore brand new possibilities resides in all of us because we have the mind of Christ (1 Corinthians 2:16) and we are made in the image of a creative God (Genesis 1:26-27).

To release this creativity we need to open up our thinking. Most of us have developed either discipline or hesitancy in our thinking. We *discipline* our thinking so we keep focus on the important responsibilities of life. We *hesitate* in our thinking because of past mistakes or fear of letting unhealthy desires take over. We need to get beyond these barriers when truly new solutions are necessary. The steps to unleash this creativity include:

Step 1: Brainstorm a solution list. Write down every possible solution you can imagine. Include ideas that seem ridiculous, absurd, and impossible. It is vital during this process that you do not analyze any of these ideas. The brainstorming process is designed to break through the barriers that have developed during your journey in life. If you analyze or evaluate ideas during the brainstorming process, you will eliminate ideas that could lead to new solutions. The goal here is to get as many ideas on paper as you possibly can in the hope that a new possibility surfaces. If you have difficulty making a large enough list, ask trusted friends to add their ideas.

Do not rush this step. You may want to take breaks and come back to your list a number of times in order to consider the greatest number of ideas. Once the brainstorm list is completed, set it aside for a time. This break can last from a few minutes to a few days. The goal of this break is to shift from a brainstorming mentality to an evaluation mentality.

Step 2: Eliminate the ridiculous ideas. Cross out any ideas that are truly ridiculous. Be careful you don't eliminate ideas that *feel* ridiculous to you but are actually good possibilities. Again, you may want to ask friends to help you figure this out. You allowed these ridiculous ideas to appear on your list to expand your creativity. Now it's time to eliminate them so they don't create clutter as you move forward.

Step 3: Eliminate ideas you are clearly not ready to consider. Some ideas on your list may sound possible, but you know in your heart you would never implement them. These ideas may not match your personality or your maturity level. Be careful that you do not eliminate these simply based on your emotional reaction to them. Real change is hard and makes you uncomfortable, so you want to keep challenging ideas on your list. You want to give yourself the freedom, however, to get rid of ideas that you are confident would make you miserable. For instance, I do not have the personality of a salesman. There are many sales positions I can imagine putting on my brainstorming list if I were considering a career change, but at this point I would eliminate most of these because selling something I'm not passionate about would wear me out.

The ideas you want to eliminate in this step are those that you know in your heart you would never focus on well enough to succeed. You do not want to commit yourself to a course of failure. It is wise to have someone you trust help you work through this step so you don't get rid of ideas you may be afraid of but that you would likely succeed at if you pursued them. Since your trusted friends are not afraid of the same things you are, they often have sharper insight into new possibilities for you.

Step 4: Walk the best ideas from your brainstorm list through the Priority Test. Once you have refined your brainstorm list, you will be left with one or more new courses of action. You now need to evaluate these ideas. Since you would do this much work only for a life-changing decision, you want to give this process the focus and time it deserves. If you have more than one idea to pursue, work the process until you have two options remaining. Then create an idea 1/idea 2 list. List the pros and cons for each, prioritize the reasons, and focus your evaluation on the high-priority reasons.

You are a decision-maker and you can figure out the journey ahead.

Just for Fun

A clergyman, a doctor, and a business consultant were playing golf together and waiting for a slow group ahead.

"What's with these people?" the business consultant exclaimed. "We've been waiting over half an hour. It's a complete disgrace."

"They're hopeless," the doctor agreed. "I've never seen such a rabble on a golf course."

The clergyman spotted the approaching greenkeeper. "What's happening with that group ahead of us?" he asked. "They're surely too slow and useless to be playing, aren't they?"

The greenkeeper replied, "Oh, yes, that's a group of blind firefighters. They lost their sight saving our clubhouse from a fire last year, so we always let them play for free anytime."

The three golfers fell silent for a moment. Then the clergyman said, "Oh dear, that's so sad. I shall say some special prayers for them tonight."

The doctor added, rather meekly, "That's a good thought. I'll get in touch with an ophthalmic surgeon friend of mine to see if there's anything that can be done for them."

After pondering the situation for a few seconds, the business consultant turned to the greenkeeper and asked, "Why can't they play at night?"[6]

Chapter 2

Decide to Seek an Adventure

"Feed your faith, and your fears will starve to death."

—ANONYMOUS[1]

Throughout the Bible, God calls men out. God initiates the call, lays down the challenge, and dares men to follow. These calls are steps of faith that bring men to the end of their abilities where they must cry out to God for help. The purpose is to get us as men to engage in pursuits that are bigger than ourselves.

It would be more efficient if men were motivated to calmly analyze their options and choose the ones that give the greatest return with the least amount of risk. This is just not how men operate. Men thrive on challenges and competition that make life an adventure rather than a routine. This sense of adventure is unique to each of us based on our abilities, giftedness, and interests. Most of us have options to choose from, and the key is to decide on the option we are most passionate about.

For instance, I love to work with my hands and I enjoy athletics, but my adventure in life is to help as many people as possible grow in their four most important relationships: with God, with their spouse (if married), with their kids, and with their circle of influence. I can do this through church ministry, writing books, speaking at conferences, personal coaching, casual conversations, father/son trips, media appearances, and more. The pursuit is big enough to be expressed in numerous ways, and it is so big I will never fully accomplish it. It will always call for my attention and stimulate my imagination as I reach out for new ways to help people grow.

For some men, their pursuit is to work with their hands. For others it involves technology. For still others it may revolve around music or literature or having influence in the lives of others. The stage is different for each of us, but the need is the same for all of us. We need to have a pursuit that is bigger than we are.

A sizeable adventure in a man's life promotes humility, produces motivation, and pushes him to personal growth. This is why God calls us out. He wants us to be humble, energetic, focused, and fascinated. When you consider that men without an adventure tend to grow bored or angry, deciding to pursue an adventure becomes more than just another option. A bored or angry man tends to make selfish decisions, develops bad habits, and puts undue strain on his relationships.

God Calls Men Out

I said earlier that we see examples throughout the Bible of men who are called out to live adventurous lives. These adventures were the idea of the God who created these men to live big lives. We won't look at every instance where this occurred, but I want to give you enough examples to see that it is normal for God to lead men on adventures that challenge them to trust God, grow stronger, seek wisdom, and cry out in aggressive humility.

Abraham's GPS

Let's first look at Abraham. He was born Abram about 1800 BC in the city of Ur in Babylonia (current day Iraq). He grew up as a city-dweller, and Jewish tradition holds that his father, Terah, was a businessman who sold idols.[2] He experienced many of the ups and downs of normal life. His brother, Haran, died while they were living in Ur. Haran's son, Lot, became Abram's responsibility and part of his family (Genesis 12:4-5). Sometime after this event, Terah set out with the family with the intention of moving to Canaan. When they came to a city named Haran, they settled there until Terah died at the age of 205 (Genesis 11:24-32). Abram was now 75 years old, used to city living, had buried his dad, and was now in charge of the family.

Then God called him out. In Genesis 12:1-5, God said to Abram, "Leave your country, your people and your father's household and go to the land I will show you." God did give him a promise to help motivate him—"I will make you into a great nation and I will bless you"—but He left out all the significant details. All the questions were a challenge.

"Where are we going, God?"

"I will show you."

God committed Himself to be Abraham's personal GPS. Turn by turn, trail by trail, day by day, God would lead him to the land that belonged to him and his family.

"When am I supposed to leave?"

"Right away."

By the way, Abram lived to be 175, so his age at this time (75) puts him in the category of a mid-life man, which means he was probably proficient in his career, in accomplishing his goals, and in handling the demands placed on him.

"Who's going to tell my wife?"

"You are, Abram."

"When she asks me why we're doing this, what am I supposed to tell her?"

"Tell her God told you to."

"Is there anything else I can tell her, or is that it?"

"Nope, that's it. But I will bless you."

Now there is a challenge few of us would come up with on our own. Change your whole life with few answers for your wife. We aren't told the details of the conversation he had with Sarai or any of the other members of his family, but we do know that he took the dare, moved his family, and accepted the change from city-dwelling to nomadic living. To be sure, he was not perfect in his obedience, but his response to the call changed history. From this moment forward, God is frequently referred to as the God of Abraham (Genesis 31:42; Exodus 3:6; 1 Kings 18:36; Acts 3:13).

The Authority of Moses

Let's move forward to Moses. His birth was miraculous and his childhood was privileged. He should have died as an infant since Pharaoh had decreed that all newborn Jewish boys be killed. But God spared his life through the intervention of Pharaoh's daughter, who found him floating in a basket in the Nile. He learned about the God of Abraham from his mom, since Pharaoh's daughter had entrusted Moses to her care. As a member of Pharaoh's household, he received an excellent education as an Egyptian prince. As a result, his confidence was high, his mind was mature, and his sense of destiny was overstated. At 40 years old he went into action to save a fellow Hebrew, but his efforts were misunderstood and his people refused to trust him.

In disgrace and discouragement, he fled from his high position. He is like many of us who had high aspirations and idealistic dreams early in life. He was going to be a leader of a great movement, and he was going to be proud of his achievements. Then his dream evaporated. The opportunities he planned for were no longer possible. His resources were depleted, his network was destroyed, and his confidence was decimated. He left the life he had spent 40 years building to start over on the back side of the desert.

Uneventfully, he rebuilt his life. He married, had a family, and built a successful shepherding business. Few people knew who he was, and his ordinary business was not going to make him famous or influential. He had resigned himself to living out his ordinary, unremarkable life.

Then God appeared to him in a burning bush (Exodus 3). It was an ordinary day, just like all the other ordinary days Moses had experienced as a shepherd. He wasn't looking for anything special to happen, but God had different plans. Again, God initiated the meeting as "the angel of the LORD appeared to him in flames of fire from within a bush" (v. 2). In astonishment, Moses said to himself, "I will go over and see this strange sight" (v. 3). After God spoke to Moses from the bush and told him that He had seen the misery of the Israelites and intended to rescue them, He then called Moses out: "So now, go. I am sending you to Pharaoh to bring my people the Israelites out of Egypt" (v. 10).

In a moment, Moses was transported from his comfortable, uneventful life to an adventure that was much bigger than he could ever have imagined. In an outburst of bewilderment, Moses asked, "Who am I, that I should go to Pharaoh and bring the Israelites out of Egypt?" (v. 11). I guess so. How many shepherds would have the confidence to confront the Pharaoh and tell him how to run his kingdom? It is kind of like trying to imagine a plumber instructing the president of the United States about how to run the country's economy.

Moses was instantly humbled and desperate for God to explain Himself. The thought of going to the most powerful leader on earth, to a country that represented failure for him, was more than he could process. Just as He had done with Abraham, God encouraged Moses with a series of promises that made the humanly impossible adventure possible.

Moses thought he was done with Egypt, but it turned out he was just in a really long warm-up period. The last person anyone expected to give commands to the Egyptian ruler was the man who had run away in disgrace. In response to God's call, Moses faced down Pharaoh, initiated the plagues in Egypt, led the nation of Israel to freedom, parted the Red Sea, and met with God face-to-face on Mount Sinai. It took 80 years to get ready for his adventure, but the impact of his journey has been felt by every generation since.

The Testing of Gideon

Gideon had grown used to being disadvantaged. When we first meet him, he's hiding wheat from the Midianite invaders (Judges 6:11). He's operating his business in secret because he's convinced these oppressors of Israel will steal what he has if they find out. He thinks he's a victim, and he is making decisions as a victim.

God's assessment of Gideon is that he is a "mighty warrior" (v. 12). Gideon's assessment of himself is much different: "How can I save Israel? My clan is the weakest in Manasseh, and I am the least in my family" (v. 15). Gideon isn't interested in an adventure; he's convinced that an adventure is nothing more than an empty dream. But God designed him for a specific purpose, so He calls Gideon out.

Gideon found himself in an emotional bind because God said such remarkable things about him. He believed God must have a plan for him, but he had limited confidence that it could actually be so. In response, he presented God with a test. He laid out a wool fleece two nights in a row. One night he asked that the fleece be wet while the ground was dry. The next night he asked that the ground be wet while the fleece was dry. God patiently participated in the test because He was committed to lead Gideon on the adventure He had designed.

In Judges 7, God presented Gideon with a test of His own. Gideon was camped with his army ready to do battle with the Midianites, and God said to him,

> "You have too many men for me to deliver Midian into their hands. In order that Israel may not boast against me that her own strength has saved her, announce now to the people, 'Anyone who trembles with fear may turn back and leave Mount Gilead.'" So twenty-two thousand men left, while ten thousand remained (Judges 7:3).

God wanted to prove to Gideon that he truly was a mighty warrior and that this ability came directly from God. He therefore reduced the size of Gideon's army from 32,000 to 10,000. I imagine Gideon was not pleased with this move, but he probably still took confidence in the 10,000 men who remained to fight.

However, since Gideon had tested God twice, God decided to test Gideon a second time. He announced that there were still too many men, and He whittled the army down to 300 (vv. 4-8). Talk about an adventure. Gideon now had 300 men to carry out a task designed for 32,000. The odds were impossible, the chances of success were unimaginable, and the call was as clear as it could possibly be.

Gideon must have been convinced by the presence and promises of God because his attitude seems to have been transformed. He confidently commanded his men to arm themselves for battle with a trumpet and a clay pot, apparently believing that God would somehow use these instruments to deliver Israel. I think he probably concluded that musical instruments and pottery were no more ridiculous than going to battle with just 300 men. He decided to embrace the adventure and won the most memorable battle of his life (Judges 7:8-25). Not only did he have an incredible story to tell his kids and grandkids, but every generation since has reveled in the possibilities that exist when God calls us out.

The Disciples' Catering Business

In Luke 9, the disciples participated with Jesus in a day-long crusade. They taught the crowds, healed the sick, and ministered to the masses. Late in the afternoon, the disciples began to realize a problem was brewing. Five thousand men had brought their families, and nobody had eaten all day. They were trying to be helpful, so they approached their rabbi: "Send the crowd away so they can go to the surrounding villages and countryside and find food and lodging, because we are in a remote place here" (v. 12).

The next statement is shocking. Jesus replied, "You give them something to eat."

The disciples had no food, no animals, and no place to go shopping. They had nothing to work with, and yet Jesus told them to solve the problem. The adventure was on. The men now had a challenge to work on that was way beyond their abilities. They had two options. They could retreat from the challenge in defeat or they could face the challenge head on and see what God did with it.

I am sure they felt overwhelmingly inadequate. I am sure they brainstormed among themselves ways to address the need. I am sure they concluded they were going to need Jesus' help in a big way if these people were going to get even a measly snack, let alone a meal.

Jesus called, so they decided to take a run at it. They went through the crowd to see what they could come up with. They scrambled around and finally came up with five loaves of bread and two fish. They had the equivalent of two lunches with 12,000 to 15,000 people to feed. The need is huge. The resources are scarce. The adventure is about to get large.

I believe this is where most of us live. God has challenged us to be good citizens, dedicated career men, committed volunteers, trustworthy husbands, invested fathers, faithful friends, and influential role models. While we entertain these lofty goals, our evaluation of our talents and resources leaves only one conclusion: The need is way bigger than my ability, and yet God has called me to this. If Jesus doesn't get involved here, intensely involved, failure is guaranteed.

The Bible doesn't tell us the attitude or the posture of the disciples as they approached Jesus, but I think they were a little embarrassed by what they had to offer. They knew they didn't have enough. Jesus knew they didn't have enough. A kindergartener would have known they didn't have enough. But it was all they had.

The difference was that Jesus had called them out to do this, and so it was part of the great adventure He had for them. Jesus took their scant resources and added His abundant resources to them. In the end, everyone ate until they were satisfied, and every disciple collected a basket of leftovers.

Our resources are simply the starting investment that proves we have accepted the challenge. What drives the adventure in our lives are the resources of Jesus that make us "more than conquerors" (Romans 8:37) and overcomers (1 John 4:4) "so that you may become blameless and pure, children of God without fault in a crooked and depraved generation" (Philippians 2:15). We cannot do it on our own, but we dare not run from it because it is how God works in our lives.

The Disciples' Travel Agency

The last example I share with you is found in Matthew 28:18-20. The key to understanding the magnitude of this adventure is that the disciples were not world travelers. They were born in Israel, lived in Israel, and probably had not traveled outside Israel. They did have contact with many nations of the world because their home base was Capernaum. This strategic city, located on the northern bank of the Sea of Galilee, was on the main trade route between Syria and Egypt. It was common for people of many cultures to gather in its streets and share their stories. The disciples, however, had only heard the stories. They had not actually traveled to these lands. Then Jesus called them out with the statement, "make disciples of all nations."

Jesus designed the challenge and initiated the conversation. The disciples simply needed to decide if they would take on the adventure of reaching the entire world with the greatest message on earth. They didn't have the money to pull it off. They didn't have the experience to pull it off. They didn't have the creativity or leadership ability to pull it off. But they did have the clear call of God and His promise to be with them.

The fact that you have heard the gospel of Christ is evidence that these men lived out the adventure. Eleven ordinary men spearheaded a movement that has impacted the entire world.

These biblical examples illustrate how God works in the hearts of men. He calls us to a challenge that is based on His abilities and promises to be with us each step of the way. It is our choice to put in our resources even though they are inadequate to meet the need. It is His choice to add His resources so that the impact of our lives is way beyond our talent.

So how do you discover the adventure God has for you?

Mark the Markers

Your personal discovery begins with taking inventory of the spiritual markers in your life. God has been orchestrating His adventure in your life for years. As you look back, you will notice significant moments in your life. Whether you grew up in a healthy or an unhealthy home, the markers were there all along the way. These markers may be moments of unusual understanding, trends of influence, or the obvious impact of certain skills in your life.

Let me illustrate this with my oldest son, Brock. Early in his life he showed a love for athletics. He would spend hours playing basketball in the driveway all by himself. He competed in a variety of youth sports growing up, and he excelled in them all. When he entered eighth grade, he decided to give football a try, and it was obvious to me that he had found his love. His first head coach was a friend of ours, and he told me before the season, "I know Brock wants to play linebacker, but I need him to play quarterback for us because he's the only one on the team who can think." Well, he took to the position like a hunter in a Bass Pro Shop. He just couldn't get enough. He played football video games. He watched multiple games on the weekends. He read articles about different defenses.

He started on the freshman football team the next year, and early in the season he threw an interception to the inside linebacker. After the game, he asked me what he could have done differently to avoid the interception.

"Well, when you rolled out what did you see?" I asked him.

"I saw the cornerback follow the split end up the sideline, and I caught a glimpse of the safety dropping back. I also noticed that the outside linebacker was chasing our running back as he ran a swing route toward the sideline. I figured the tight end would be open, but the inside linebacker moved faster than I expected."

"You saw all that?" I said to him in astonishment.

"Yeah."

My only response was, "You're doing just fine. Just keep playing. I'm sure you're going to have a good high school career."

When he got to college, he called home to tell me, "Five guys are competing for the starting quarterback role. I know how this will play out. For the first few weeks of practice we'll be even. But by the first game, I'll establish myself as the smartest guy on the field and get the opportunity to start."

I thought he was a little too cocky, but it played out just as he said it would.

As I considered these moments in his football experience, I began to conclude that this young man was born to be a football coach who would influence young men throughout his life. I mentioned it to Brock, but he was determined to get a business degree and be a businessman. I didn't argue, but I did continue to pray. Every once in a while I would suggest that he stay open to the idea of coaching, but I got the same response every time: "Thanks for your confidence, Dad, but I'm going to run my own business."

After playing four years in college, he decided to try out for an Arena Football League team to see if he could play the game he loved a few more years before he started his business career. While he waited for the tryout, he volunteered to help out with the high school team in his hometown, and the bug got him. From the first week on the field, he discovered he loved coaching. He is now an offensive coordinator and teaches business classes in high school because he paid attention to the markers.

It's Your Turn

What markers are you aware of in your life? What moments of unusual understanding have you experienced? What trends of influence have you noticed in your interactions with others? What obvious impact have your skills had in your life?

Grab the Gift

Since the birth of the church, every believer in Christ has been given a spiritual gift (Romans 12:4-8; 1 Corinthians 12:7-11; Ephesians

4:7-13), and your adventure revolves around your giftedness. At first your gift may seem like the other talents you have, but over time you will notice that this skill has a more enduring impact than the other abilities you have. When this gift is operational, perspective in life changes, hearts soften, interest in Jesus grows, decisions are made, and people are encouraged. The impact of these pursuits can be attributed only to the supernatural work of the Holy Spirit, and it makes sense to grab the opportunities these gifts present to us.

The best way I know to identify your giftedness is to put yourself in action. Try out pursuits that interest you, and see what God does. It takes some honest humility to make this work because we tend to give ourselves more credit than we deserve in the areas we are most interested in. I know of a few men who are convinced they have the gift of teaching, but no one seems to have the gift of learning from them. I also know of some men who proclaim they have gifts in fixing things, but everything they fix needs to be re-fixed. It's a sign of maturity when you admit you're not good at some things. It frees you up to focus on those areas where God moves best in your life.

I should be good at water skiing. I have been athletic my whole life, and I have good balance. It stands to reason that waterskiing would come naturally. Reality is a little different. I organized a day of water skiing for a group of friends, which included a double amputee. He lost half his left leg and half his left arm in a motorcycle accident. He's a fighter, however, and learned how to snow ski after his accident. He agreed to come to our ski fest, but he was running late.

I wanted to get up on one ski this day, since I'd never been able to do this. After several attempts without success, I grabbed the rope one more time, and then yelled to the boat operator to "hit it." The boat accelerated, yanking my exhausted arms forward and smashing all eight fingernails on the ski. The pain was awful, and the big bruise on my ego was worse.

I got dropped off on the lakeshore, found a quiet spot, and nursed my wounded fingers. Then my friend showed up. He sat next to me, took off his prosthetic leg, hopped over to the water with his custom ski, and called the boat over. He slipped on the ski, launched from the shore, and took two laps around the lake. He then performed a perfectly executed shore landing, took off his ski, and hopped back over to my pathetic party. I wanted to hit him when he said, "So Bill, how are you doing?" It didn't seem appropriate to say, "I can't believe I was just ridiculously shown up by a guy with one arm and one leg," so I just said, "Fine, thanks for asking. Hey, great ride." It's been a lot easier on me since I admitted that I'm not much of a skier.

It also takes a lot of humility to admit that we're really good at some things because God empowers us. Of course we are talented in these areas because God is awesome in everything He does. You probably know some men who are gifted communicators. They teach classes or Bible studies and have a knack for making the information come alive. These gifts are easy to identify, but only a few men get them. The behind-the-scenes gifts are much more common.

I remember the first time I encountered a man who was gifted by God as a handyman. He was a retired plumber, and something special took place whenever he worked on a project. He approached each project with uncommon grace. He never seemed rushed, rarely got frustrated, and appeared to be devoid of stress. Any of us that assisted him learned how to be better at working with our hands, and we found ourselves in significant discussions about life, God, and the people who meant the most to us. We were usually unaware of the depth of the conversation until we were well into it. He acted as though it was no big deal, but none of us could re-create the impact he had when he worked with his hands. Everyone who knew Harold recognized the gift.

You are similarly gifted in some area. If you try different opportunities and stay alert to the times when people are unusually affected by your words or actions, you will begin to recognize the gifts God has given you. It may be in musical expression or in helping others grasp important concepts. It may be in administration or accounting or acting. The truth is that you have been spiritually empowered in a specific way so that your life can have an impact that is bigger than your efforts.

I recognized in my late twenties that I was gifted as a pastor/teacher. I love to help people grow as they apply the truth of God's Word to their lives. Every time I see someone grasp a biblical concept and start living it out, I experience deep satisfaction. This is one of the discoveries that led me to the conclusion that my life is all about helping people grow in their relationships.

If you are struggling to identify your gifts, a few online inventories can assist you. Among them are:

- http://buildingchurch.net/g2s.htm
- www2.elca.org/evangelizingchurch/assessments/spiritgifts.html
- www.churchgrowth.org/cgi-cg/gifts.cgi?intro=1

You may want to visit one of these sites and work through the process to sharpen your focus.

Pursue Your Passion

God created us with high levels of testosterone in our bodies. This amazing hormone makes us aggressive, strong, and competitive. When we find something we love to do, we pursue it with all our might. We love to solve problems and avoid situations that seem to have no point. We like to think our way through life, but we also like to feel life in the gut. When we find pursuits that stimulate the mind and energize the body, we explode with motivation. This is why men who love their jobs work really hard at them, men who love their hobbies spend long hours enjoying them, and men who find a talent they love will do what it takes to excel at it. Conversely, men who don't love what they do grow bored, agitated, and selfish.

It's so important for each of us as men to have an adventure to pursue that captures our imagination, ignites our soul, and drives us to grow. God put a passion in you to drive you toward the adventure He has designed for you. But passion is not sufficient alone to define the path we ought to follow. You are just as aware as I am of how quickly the passions of our lives can get out of control and grow self-destructive. History is littered with stories of highly influential, remarkably talented men who cashed in their influence for the allure of power, wealth, or sexual pleasure. At the same time, no man ever left his mark on the world without a driving passion for something. Passion is a powerful force in our souls, so it cannot be allowed to just run wild. It must be treated like a powerful engine in a powerful vehicle.

I had the opportunity to drive a Porsche 911, and I will never be the same. A rumble went through my entire body when I started the engine and it growled back at me in enthusiasm. Before the car even moved, I had a clear sense that this was a machine to be respected.

I put the car in gear and pushed on the throttle. It responded eagerly as if it were begging me to let it go faster. I turned onto a winding road and headed into a turn with a sign marked 25 mph. This nimble machine accelerated throughout the entire turn and exited the other side going 60 mph. I had a strong sense that I could have gone faster. I began to realize this automobile would accept as much throttle as I was willing to give it and that I needed to manage the throttle wisely. Otherwise, this car would just keep going faster until it reached a point that I could no longer control it.

I then turned onto a three-lane road with a long straightaway. I downshifted, changed lanes quickly, and stepped on the accelerator to find out how fast this car really was. The car quickly shot forward. Just as quickly, I saw the police car at an intersection half a mile ahead. I let off the throttle and pressed on the brake just enough to bring the car a little under the speed limit. Without a willingness to put the brakes on, all this power would surely have cost me a hefty price.

After getting my feet back on the ground, I realized I had just learned some important skills for handling the passions God has placed in my heart. First of all, *I need to respect the power.* The passions that God has placed in me can take me to exhilarating heights with exciting opportunities. When I'm pursuing an area of life I'm passionate about, motivation is easy, commitment is attractive, and the results are rewarding. Second, I realized that *I need to control the throttle.* Our passions will accept as much throttle as we're willing to give them. They just want expression, and they will keep driving us further and faster until we let off the gas. Our passions are great motivators, but they do not think on their own. Third, *there are times when we must put on the brakes.* Our passions are intent on creating movement in life, and they consistently call us to do more. But sometimes doing more is not the right move. Not everything is fun and exciting. Much of life is just responsibility. It must be done, it must be done daily, and it must be done with discipline or all of life becomes unmanageable.

Beware of the Dark Side

While our passions are great motivators, they are not discerning, so they can get us in trouble quickly. Everything you do well has a dark side to it. Sexual love in marriage can be corrupted into lust and self-indulgence. Aggressiveness can turn to anger and manipulation. Strength can easily be counterfeited by self-effort and self-reliance. Success can be transformed into pride that makes men believe they are exempt from the rules that apply to the rest of us.

This is why the Bible calls us to be alert (1 Thessalonians 5:4-8; 1 Peter 5:8-9). We are at war with ourselves and with the enemy of our souls. Our lower nature is consistently tempted to cross over to the dark side of life to engage in self-defeating pleasures. Satan and his army are prowling our world looking for men to victimize. If these two ever get in sync, the damage is incredible.

Men who are alert are ready to spring into action whenever it is required of them. It doesn't mean that we should be workaholics or constantly nervous about what will happen next. We are to have the readiness of a soldier or an athlete who does not know exactly what will happen next, but he has trained his body, mind, and will to respond to the expected and the unexpected.

We don't want to be afraid of our passions just because they have the potential to create damage anymore than we want to avoid driving because there are dangers on the road. We just need a plan for staying on the road. The road signs are posted in 1 John 2:16. Be alert for:

"The cravings of sinful man." These represent the lustful impulses that spring from the fallen nature that resides within us all. When these temptations assault us, the strategic response is to run away (1 Corinthians 6:18). I know this doesn't sound manly, but it is the best response. Running into a fire praying that the flames won't burn you is beyond ridiculous, and yet men have been doing this with their moral lives for centuries. When your cravings chase you, run faster.

"The lust of the eyes." This is equivalent to materialism. There has always been an illusion that happiness can be achieved through money and possessions. Mankind is ingenious and remarkably resourceful. As a result, our world is filled with innovations, gadgets, entertainment options, machines, and collectibles. If your heart is not solidly focused

on Jesus, these inventions become distractions that draw your heart away from a vibrant relationship with the living God in exchange for a static relationship with inanimate objects. If this is your temptation, it's time to intensify your relationship with Jesus. More time spent in the spiritual disciplines and worship will draw your heart back to your Creator and away from the created things that are trying to take His place.

"The boasting of what we have and do." This is the age-old battle with pride. We get too impressed with ourselves and our accomplishments. We mistakenly think that the power we harness on earth is impressive enough to be compared with God's high position. We begin to believe that we are the solution to our problems and that we have all the resources we need for life.

If you're tempted to believe that you are the source of your greatness, it's time to serve others. Jesus said, "The greatest among you will be your servant" (Matthew 23:11). As you serve others, you gain perspective into your humble state, and you gain appreciation for what God has done for you. If you are prone to think highly of yourself, you are probably talented. It would be unrealistic to tell you that you're not that great because you have evidence to the contrary. When you serve others, however, you realize that all your talent cannot force the hearts of others to soften. Your talent combined with God's softening work causes transformation in the lives of others. Without God's part, your talent has little to no effect in the areas of life that matter most.

Don't let the dangers of the road distract you from living out your adventure.

It's Your Turn

Describe the adventure God has for your life as you understand it today.

Just for Fun

George W. Bush was invited to address the graduating class of 2001 at his alma mater, Yale University. To remind them all that they have possibilities he said, "To those of you who received honors, awards, and distinctions, I say, well done. And to the C students, I say, you too can be president of the United States."[3]

Chapter 3

Decide to Be Competitive

"If winning isn't everything, why do they keep score?"

—Vincent Lombardi[1]

In 2009, I attended a football game at Mississippi State University and noticed a large construction project just getting started at one end of the field. I asked the couple who invited us to the game, "What's going on at the end of the field?"

"Oh, that's the new scoreboard. The University of Mississippi ordered a new scoreboard that was going to be the largest in the SEC. We waited until theirs was ordered, and then we ordered one just a little bigger. Now we're going to have the largest scoreboard in the SEC."

"I should have known."

Life is a competitive venture, and men are engineered for competition. We have larger muscles than our female counterparts. We have higher levels of testosterone, and our brains are wired to narrow the options and focus on the most successful course of action. God created us this way. We must contend against spiritual forces that are bent on destroying lives. We must wrestle against a world system that tends to control and manipulate. And we must compete with our own tendencies to engage in self-destructive thoughts and behaviors. If you want to maximize your life, therefore, you'll want to embrace that life is a competition.

Life Is Filled with Challenges

Many times Jesus put His disciples into situations that forced them to be competitive. One of the clearest is at the end of Mark 4 and the beginning of Mark 5. Jesus had spent the day teaching people at the

Sea of Galilee, and a large crowd had gathered, large enough that He had to get in a boat and teach from the water.

After the long day, He met alone with His disciples and helped them grasp the meaning of the parables He had taught. Then "when evening came, he said to his disciples, 'Let us go over to the other side'" (Mark 4:35). It sounded like an ordinary, innocent request. They had crossed the sea numerous times without incident. To intensify the conclusion that this wasn't going to be a big deal, Jesus moved to the stern of the boat and went to sleep. The disciples must have thought to themselves, *It's been a good day. We accomplished a lot, and now it's time to relax, regroup, and rest.*

They had no idea that Jesus was sending them into a severe storm followed by an encounter with a demon-possessed man. Life was about to transform from calm to competitive.

Life is filled with challenges. The storm the disciples faced erupted quickly. It's described as "a furious squall" with waves so large they began to fill the boat with water. With little warning, it was time to compete with nature for their survival. Game on.

Mike Krzyzewski, head basketball coach for Duke University, tells his teams, "If a team cannot perform with excellence at a moment's notice, they probably will fail in the long run."[2] Hockey coach Scotty Bowman echoes this same thought: "I found out that if you are going to win games, you had better be ready to adapt."[3]

Out of necessity, the disciples immediately kicked into gear, bailing water as fast as they could. To their astonishment, they noticed that their leader was still asleep. Frantic, they woke Him up and accused Him of not caring about the danger they were in. Jesus calmly "got up, rebuked the wind and said to the waves, 'Quiet! Be still!'" (v. 39). And immediately the wind died down and it became calm.

He then asked them, "Why are you so afraid? Do you still have no faith?" (v. 40). Those *who are afraid* of the challenges before them tend to hold back and hesitate, which leads to indecision and sometimes injury. Those *who do not believe* they can defeat the challenges find ways to sabotage their success. Therefore, every successful coach addresses the need for his athletes to eliminate fear and visualize their accomplishments until they are convinced they will happen.

Consider these wise words about responding positively to challenges:

- "Do not fear the winds of adversity. Remember: A kite rises against the wind rather than with it."—Anonymous[4]
- "Whether you think you can or think you can't, you're right."—Henry Ford[5]
- "You have to expect things of yourself before you can do them."—Michael Jordan[6]
- "You need to play with supreme confidence, or else you'll lose again, and then losing becomes a habit." —Joe Paterno[7]
- "How do you go from where you are to where you want to be? I think you have to have an enthusiasm for life. You have to have a dream, a goal, and you have to be willing to work for it."—Jim Valvano, basketball coach[8]
- "I always won in my imagination. I always hit the game-winning shot, or I hit the free throw. Or if I missed, there was a lane violation, and I was given another one." —Mike Krzyzewski[9]
- "Do not let what you cannot do interfere with what you can do."—John Wooden[10]
- "I learned that if you want to make it bad enough, no matter how bad it is, you can make it."—Gale Sayers[11]
- "No pressure, no diamonds."—Unknown[12]

Challenges Are Meant to Be Overcome

It would have been enough had Jesus stopped after calming the sea, but the contests of life do not fit into nice neat boxes. As soon as the boat arrived on the shore, a new challenge interrupted their day. Of course, Jesus knew this challenge was waiting for them, and He willingly kept on course because He wanted His disciples to grow in their ability to face obstacles to their faith.

Let me set the scene. Approximately one-quarter of a mile inland from where they landed on the eastern shore of the Sea of Galilee was a steep cliff that led up to a plateau. The cliff was decorated with limestone caverns and rock chambers where the dead were buried and where demonized people lived. On top of the plateau was a grazing area for a herd of swine.

As the boat landed, the most severely demonized man from the caverns ran toward them shouting in his loudest voice. I can only imagine the reaction of the disciples. This man was dirty, daunting, and dangerous. His history proved that he was a hopeless case. "No one could bind him any more, not even with a chain…No one was strong enough to subdue him" (Mark 5:3,4). When confronted, this man referred to himself as Legion. A legion was the principle unit of the Roman army and comprised several thousand warriors. In Jewish teaching, *legion* refers to a group of hurtful spirits who lie in wait for men to do them harm. This demonized man was the last person the disciples wanted to help, let alone have any contact with, and Jesus strategically had them land the boat right in front of his neighborhood. Game on.

In this contest, the disciples are merely in training. In the future, they will be required to heal the sick, free those in bondage, and overcome extreme challenges, but this day they are going to watch their master in action.

The drama was high in this confrontation. The evil spirits began the wrestling match knowing they were serious underdogs to the Son of God. The best they could do was engage in smack talk. "What do you want with us? Swear to God you won't torture us. I know, send us into that herd of pigs." So Jesus allowed the evil spirits to go into the herd of about 2000 pigs, and the porkers panicked. The snorting and the pounding of hooves was no doubt deafening as they "rushed down the steep bank into the lake" (v. 13).

The impact of Jesus' authority over this man and the evil spirits forced everyone in that region to make a choice. When Jesus and the disciples got back into the boat, "the man who had been demon-possessed begged to go with him" (v. 18). This man had experienced the transforming power of Jesus firsthand, and he wanted to be with Him, serve with Him, and compete with Him for the lives of others. He was disappointed when Jesus said, "Go home to your family and tell them," but he accepted the challenge and began to tell others what God had done for him. As a result of his willingness to enter the game, "all the people were amazed" (v. 20). This was the bigger picture. Jesus set this man free so he could influence others to live free also.

The mere spectators, on the other hand, grew afraid and refused to get in the game. Those who tended the pigs ran off to report their loss to others. A crowd of people gathered to see what had happened and exposed the lack of courage in their hearts. "When they saw the man…dressed and in his right mind…they were afraid" (v. 15). Wow. This man had been set free from the demons that tormented him, and it scared people. They had grown accustomed to his disastrous state, and they wanted anything but change. Rather than get attracted to the possibilities that existed in competing alongside Jesus, they ran from the challenge and retreated into their seemingly safe, comfortable existence. In a sad declaration of defeat, "the people began to plead with Jesus to leave their region" (v. 17).

Competitors or Spectator?

These are just a couple of the stories from the life of Jesus that reveal that life is a competition. Add to this the bold words of the apostle Paul in 1 Corinthians 9:24—"Do you not know that in a race all the runners run, but only one gets the prize? Run in such a way as to get the prize"—and you get the inescapable realization that Jesus has recruited us to be His teammates in winning over the hearts and minds of men. We must all decide if we will accept the challenge or sit in the stands while others enjoy the thrill of competition.

In order for a football team to be successful, it must have a productive offense, a solid defense, and effective special teams. In similar fashion, there are three categories of pursuits in our lives as men that require us to compete in order to be winners.

Offense corresponds to *our careers*. God made us to work and to work hard. The first thing God gave Adam was a job. "The Lord God took the man and put him in the Garden of Eden to work it and take care of it" (Genesis 2:15). Before the fall, it may have been simple to make a living, but once sin entered the human experience, work has been a competitive struggle. Weeds began to grow, the ground became difficult to work, and sweat became a daily price for productivity (Genesis 3:17-19). In addition, a world system developed because of this lost battle that is counterproductive, evil by nature, and focused on fighting against what God wants for people (2 Corinthians 10:3-5; Ephesians 2:1-3; 6:10-12). It is in this environment that we earn a living. We need to strain, struggle, and stretch ourselves to reach our potential. We need to negotiate wisely, stand ground courageously, and recover quickly from setbacks. We must commit to growth in our career skills or be left behind in the race.

The foundation of all careers is competition as men strive to find the limits of their productivity. Throughout history we encounter stories of the competitive drive that has made American business the powerhouse that it is. And sometimes that competitiveness is over-the-top, literally:

> During the roaring '20s, architects William Van Alen and H. Craig Severance were commissioned to design a building at 40 Wall Street in Manhattan's financial district. When the partners split up during the project's construction, Van Alen left the firm and went uptown to work on Walter Chrysler's new skyscraper…Severance secretly had the lantern and flagpole added to the top of 40 Wall Street to make his tower the tallest. When Van Alen found out about the ruse, he countered by building a secret spire in the elevator shaft of the Chrysler Building's crown. Once Severance's tower had topped off (in November 1929), Van Alen had the spire hoisted into place: Severance's 40 Wall Street was indeed the world's tallest building—for about 90 minutes.[13]

A football team's defense corresponds to *our families*. The members of our family must be valued, protected, and guided toward their potential. Our marriages are being attacked by social policies, sagging values, and selfish priorities. If we don't contend for our wives' hearts, we leave them open to the assault. We must spend time with them, listen to them, hold them, romance them, work through decisions with them, help them feel secure, accept them, open doors of opportunity for them, and love them with all our hearts. Our kids, likewise, are being recruited by a materialistic market, a self-centered social structure, and values based on faulty reasoning. It's all packaged in attractive clothes, stunning special effects, and masterful music. The only thing standing between the hearts of our kids and the deception in our world is us. We need to pray for them, talk with them, spend time with them, help them make strong decisions, discipline them, open doors of opportunity for them, and stand in the gap when they get off track.

Our health, our homes, and our hobbies represent the special teams. These areas of life must be maintained with diligence and discipline because they all tend to deteriorate. It takes no effort to gain weight and weaken your health. It takes focused, consistent effort to stay in shape and protect your well-being. It takes no special skill to let weeds grow and paint chip. It takes planned, proactive effort to maintain your home, your yard, and any other possessions you value. Your hobbies help you maintain balance in your life and often provide your best opportunities for influencing others. If you neglect them, your skills deteriorate and your stamina diminishes. If, however, you schedule time for these pursuits, your skills continue to grow and your effort becomes more efficient.

Love the Game

So what does it take to be a competitor? First and foremost, you must love the game of life. It has been instructive to watch my boys compete in sports throughout their lives. It requires hard work and long hours. They get sore, tired, and frustrated. Year after year, however, they compete because they love the game. They will pay whatever price is necessary, and they always keep their eye on the goal of winning the next contest.

Do you love life? Does the possibility of success thrill you? Do you still feel satisfaction when you finish a project, close a deal, overcome a problem, or create a breakthrough? Does the potential of earning more, having a bigger slice of influence, being head over heels in love with your wife, or seeing your kids figure out who they are get to you? I hope so because that's how God created you. God gave you a heart so that you could love Him, love life, and love the important people in your world. "Above all else, guard your heart, for it is the wellspring of life" (Proverbs 4:23). The goal is "love, which comes from a pure heart and a good conscience and a sincere faith" (1 Timothy 1:5).

We are all born with a love for life. Just watch kids playing sometime. They are determined to have fun, they are curious without hesitation, they laugh and cry without shame, and they run into the arms of people they recognize. They dream of greatness and of worlds far, far away. Then we grow up, and if we're not careful, we lose our zest for life amidst the disappointments, defeats, and difficulties.

When I think about a man who loves life, I think of my friend Glenn who was reborn at 49. He started his career in the navy and found that it suited him, so he stayed in for 20 years. He met a young lady, fell in love, and together they set out to have a good life together. They were thrilled when they gave birth to their two sons, and they concluded that life was just the way it was supposed to be. That worked until their youngest son was about to turn 12. He was a responsible young man, so they gave him freedom to play with his friends and regulate his schedule. One day he and another friend went exploring in a wooded area near the house. The two boys were playing trucks along the wall of a dried-up creek bed. Unexpectedly, a piece of clay the size of a desk broke loose from the top of the wall 20 feet above them and hit both boys. They both passed from this earth too early for anyone to reasonably explain.

Glenn and his wife fell into a deep grief that took over their lives. Glenn spent more and more time at work while his wife spent more time away from home looking for anything that would help her sadness go away. The pain kept growing as it pushed them farther and farther from each other. He finally decided they could not continue to live like this, so he asked her for a divorce. The breakup was messy and hurtful as they projected their pain on each other every time they talked.

Glenn was now pushing 40, getting ready to get out of the navy with no wife, no family, and nothing but his will to draw on. He recovered, kind of. He bounced around a number of different jobs before joining a mortgage company. He spent most of his evenings talking with shallow friends at bars sharing a couple of drinks. He wasn't sad. He wasn't happy. He was just numb. He didn't realize he was missing something because he wasn't aware of much.

One day a colleague of his told him about the love of Jesus and the hope it had brought to his life. Glenn found this man's story interesting, and he was impressed with the energy in his life. He met with this man a couple more times just to hear more. On the fourth meeting, the man's wife asked Glenn, "Is there any reason you can think of why you don't want to ask Jesus into your life today?"

Glenn was stunned by the question, but he couldn't think of a reason to say no. He secretly wanted the energy he saw in this couple, and he figured he didn't have anything to lose, so he agreed to pray with his friends.

Glenn's life changed that day. He showed up at church the following Sunday, and you could see the hunger in his eyes. "What's the next step?" he asked. "What do I need to do to make this real?" I gave him some steps he could take to begin getting to know his Savior:

- Read your Bible daily.
- Pray about the things that are important to you.
- Come to church and get involved in a small group that will help you learn and grow.
- Whenever you have questions, write them down and ask people until you get answers.

He did everything I suggested without hesitation, and the transformation was amazing. He found a joy he didn't think would be possible after losing his son. He began to realize he had the same energy he had seen in his friends.

I asked him one morning, "Glenn, how are you doing today?"

"Well, the back of my calves really hurt," he said.

"What are you talking about?"

"Yeah, my calves just ache. Ever since I met Jesus, I've had an unstoppable bounce in my step. My calves have never worked this hard before."

One day he came to me with a catalog from a distributor of Christian books and asked, "Which of these books should I buy?" I marked 13 books that included a couple of commentaries, a survey of theology, personal discipleship manuals, and leadership books. I marked them in the order I suggested he buy them. Ten days later, he came to my office with a box containing 13 books and asked, "Okay, now what do I do with these?"

His growth was intense and persistent, and God was working in his life at a rapid pace. A year into his faith journey, he had a strong sense that he should go back to college and get his teaching credential to teach high school math. He enrolled in San Diego Christian College and enjoyed school like never before. While he was there, he attended a missions conference and met a representative from Wycliffe Bible Translators. He discovered they had a need for a teacher at a compound in Colombia, and his heart stirred within him. He signed up to serve at this school, and at the age of 52, moved to South America to begin his new career. He absolutely loved it as he taught missionary children and other Americans from the area.

He eventually met a native Colombian, fell in love, got married, and together they adopted an eight-year-old Colombian girl. He loves his life and is now pastoring a new church where he tells the story of how God found an aimless, bored, middle-aged man and transformed him into a competitor in the game of life who can't wait for his next opportunity.

Focus on Victory

Athletes in every sport compete because they want to win on game day. Life is the same way. God has called us to live in victory, and it begins with our focus. Winners think like winners.

Hebrews 12:1-3 presents our journey in life as an athletic competition. A crowd is cheering us on (saints who have lived before us), and the focal point for our race is a person: "Let us fix our eyes on Jesus, the author and perfecter of our faith, who for the joy set before him endured the cross, scorning its shame, and sat down at the right hand of the throne of God" (v. 2). First Corinthians 15:57 declares, "But thanks be to God! He gives us the victory through our Lord Jesus Christ." Paul reveals the secret that keeps him going in Philippians 3:14, "I press on toward the goal to win the prize for which God has called me heavenward in Christ Jesus."

These verses all remind us that victory begins in the mind. Competitors lose their enthusiasm when they forget why they're in the game. If you can envision your dream, you can live it with the help of Christ. If you can imagine a life worth living, you can pull the pieces together to make it happen. If you keep the goal in focus, you can figure out much easier the strategy that leads to victory.

Some experiences in our lives live forever. One of those for me happened during my senior year in high school. I was playing basketball, but the season wasn't going well. I had started as the point guard for the first half of the season, but then I sat on the bench most of the rest of the year. Becoming a support player who worked to make others better was an unfamiliar role for me. I would love to tell you that I handled it with grace and enthusiasm, but I was frustrated, lethargic, and wondering if I should even finish the season.

A good friend decided to help me stay motivated for the last half of the season. "Bill, if you score in double figures during any game the rest of the year," he said, "I'll buy you a steak dinner." I wish I could tell you that I was focused on helping my team to a league championship and the playoffs, but the reality is that I was now playing for a steak dinner. My motivation went sky high. The goal was not sufficient for any kind of high achievement, but just having a new purpose reignited my soul. With renewed enthusiasm, I got back in gear looking for my opportunity.

Game after game passed with little time on the court, so with five games left in the season, my friend approached me again and said, "Hey, Bill, I know you're frustrated. Let's change our deal. If you score in double figures *combined* for the rest of the season, I'll buy you that steak dinner."

New goal. New enthusiasm. I prayed to get into games. I went to every contest with anticipation believing I could do my part to get that dinner. Three more games passed, and my friend modified the deal one more time: "Bill, if you score I will buy you a steak dinner."

I knew that any chance at victory or fame as a basketball player was over. I would not be considered for a scholarship. I would not be considered for all-league honors. I would never be a candidate for team MVP. But I could win something, even if it was just a steak dinner. The next to last game of the year the coach put me in for 12 seconds, not even long enough to get the ball in my hands. So it all came down to the last game.

The game did not go well. We trailed the whole way, and with one and a half minutes left, it was obvious we were not going to win. So the coach put me in. I was a wild man on the floor. You would have thought we were playing for an important championship given the level of my effort. With six seconds to go, I stole the ball at half-court and raced toward the basket. It seemed as if everything was in slow motion. I could hear the crowd cheering. I could see two defenders chasing me. I jumped and was acutely aware of the ball in my outstretched hand for the layup of my life. I could see the ball falling through the net and the two seconds remaining on the clock as if it were a scene in a movie. I took off running down the sidelines, pointing at my friend in the stands, screaming enthusiastically. We had lost the game by 12 points, but I acted as though we had just won.

My layup didn't redeem the season or take the place of a league championship, but I learned an important lesson about competition. When you have a clear goal, you gain the energy to pursue victory. I got my name in the newspaper only once during my athletic pursuits. After that last game, the last line of the story read, "Bill Farrel won a bet by scoring the last two points of the season."

Learn to Love Practice

We already mentioned that in Hebrews 12:1-3, we are called to walk in victory by focusing our sights on Jesus who created our faith and has run the race before us. In verses 4-6, we get a stark reminder that most of life is practice. "You have not yet resisted to the point of shedding your blood...the Lord disciplines those he loves." Everyone who has ever accomplished anything worthwhile has spent enormous amounts of time and energy in preparation. Bobby Knight, the famous and controversial coach of Indiana and Texas Tech basketball, emphasized this to every young man who played for him: "Most people have the will to win; few have the will to prepare to win."

I've been watching athletes my whole life. The real story of their accomplishments are the hundreds of days, year after year, spent in the weight room getting stronger, countless hours doing drills on the field getting faster, thousands of miles on the track building endurance, and a ridiculous number of hours watching film and studying playbooks to prepare their minds for action.

Every champion has embraced the need to spend more time at practice than he will ever spend playing the game. He knows that his achievements are the result of drill after drill, workout after workout, film session after film session.

This is where we discover how competitive we really are. We have been entrusted with the skills, talents, and gifts to fulfill God's purpose in our lives. Bringing the plan to fruition requires faithfulness on our part, which Paul likens to athletic training: "I discipline my body and make it my slave" (1 Corinthians 9:27 NASB). Our bodies tend toward deterioration and can be kept in shape only through strenuous activity. Our minds tend toward selfish thinking and can be kept focused on truth only through diligent study. Our souls tend toward pride and laziness and can be kept motivated only through consistent reminders of God's grace. Our desires tend toward indulgence and self-destruction and can be kept under control only through accountability to the Holy Spirit and to fellow believers.

So what does a workout look like that prepares us to win? It begins with a steady diet of God's Word. There are numerous ways to ingest the Bible, and it takes consistency in all of these to maintain the spiritual and intellectual resources we need to make great decisions. Romans 10:17 reveals that part of the diet of champions is *hearing* the Bible: "Faith comes from hearing." You can accomplish this through listening to others teach God's Word, attending church regularly where God's Word is preached, and listening to an audio Bible.

Psalm 119:11 reveals that *memorization* is a vital part of our biblical diet. Righteous living develops when we hide God's Word in our heart through committing it to memory. This gets harder as we get older, but it never loses its importance.

Second Timothy 2:15 reminds us to diligently *study* the Bible so that we can be approved workmen. When the Bible was written, the authors used the common language of the day so that it would be readily understandable. It was, however, written in a different time and different culture than we live in. To harvest the principles taught so that we can integrate them into our lives, we need to diligently investigate the truth of God's Word and the cultural setting in which it was penned.

The fourth element of our diet is *reading* the Bible. In Deuteronomy 17:18-20, the king of Israel was commanded to keep a copy of God's Word with him and to "read it all the days of his life." First Thessalonians 5:27 is a New Testament example of the priority of reading the Bible as part of our spiritual journey: "I charge you before the Lord to have this letter read to all the brothers." As you read the Bible regularly, you put together the pieces of the puzzle as you see how the Old and New Testaments are tied together and how the principles of God's Word are consistent from cover to cover.

To help tie it all together, Psalm 1 challenges us to *meditate* on God's word "day and night." Meditation is the process of thinking over and over about what we have learned. The more you focus on truth, the clearer it becomes. The more you wrestle with how to live it out in your life, the more skilled you get at living biblically. So the five elements of your biblical nutrition are: *hearing, studying, reading, memorizing*, and *meditating*.

It is not enough, however, to just take truth in. Hebrews 4:12 tells us that the Word of God is "living and active." As such, "it judges the thoughts and attitudes of the heart." As you take in the Bible, a reaction begins within your soul that must be worked out or you will become spiritually bloated. We need to pay attention to God's Word and obey it as we immerse ourselves in it (James 1:22-25).

The interactive nature of the Bible causes verses to affect us in two distinct ways. The first are *verses that make us feel better* about ourselves and our lives. God uses these verses to keep us encouraged in the midst of the struggle. He knows that life is difficult and that we often get worn down and worn out, and He reminds us that He is always with us, always engaged in our journey, and always committed to "cause all things to work together for good to those who love God" (Romans 8:28). Sometimes He even causes certain verses to jump off the pages of Scripture to encourage our hearts.

But the Bible also contains *verses that bother us*. You may be confused or irritated or agitated by what you read. Perhaps the reason you have this reaction is that the passage is pointing to an area in your life God wants to change. There may be an attitude or an action or a habit that is next on God's agenda for you. He knows the time is right, so He begins to stir up your soul in preparation for another transforming experience. We often ignore these verses because they are uncomfortable. We assume we don't have the ability to understand or that Satan is trying to confuse us when in reality God is trying to get our attention for the next step of maturity. Another reason we often ignore these verses is that they aren't clear to us. Even though the passage is pointing to an area of needed growth, it may not point directly at the change. For instance, if God needs to toughen you up, stories of judgment and confrontation may bother you. Or if God wants to soften you up, you may find stories of compassion and intimacy unattractive and irritating.

The key is to pay attention to any verses you have a reaction to. When you commit to do this every time you are aware of it, Jesus becomes the coach who orchestrates your workout. He lets you know when change is necessary. He lets you know when you can relax and enjoy the progress you have already made. He lets you know when it's time to step up the intensity and focus on strenuous obedience. He points out when a bad habit is stifling your effectiveness and how to make the changes that remove the limits to your success.

For instance, the story earlier in this chapter about Jesus calming the storm has recently had a profound impact on me. Surprisingly, Jesus' words, "Why are you so afraid? Do you still have no faith?" (Mark 4:40) encouraged me. I know these were challenging questions, but having grown up in a fearful home, I rejoiced that I could say, "Thank You, Jesus, that my adult life is not ruled by fear like my childhood was." I was reminded again that His redemption in my life is real and effective.

I had a different reaction to the beginning of the next chapter in Mark's gospel. It bothered me that Jesus put His disciples into an intense confrontation with a demon-possessed man the morning after one of the hardest nights of their lives. This negative reaction surprised me also. I like to work hard, and I love being involved with ministry opportunities. The thought of a miracle at sea followed by the freeing of a tormented man sounds like a great thing, so why was this bothering me?

I don't think I have it all figured out, but one thing is obvious to me. I don't like being left out of decisions that affect my life. Intellectually, I realize this is a problem if I call Jesus Lord. Since He is in control of everything, He can make any decision He wants anytime He wants. In my mind, I want to cooperate, but I struggle accepting His right to alter my schedule.

If I want to compete in life, I need to listen to the message that I don't have to be afraid. If I want to compete at the highest level, I am going to have to cooperate with Him as He directs my schedule.

It's Your Turn

Note here any verses that you are currently reacting to.

Verses that have been encouraging me:

Verses that have been bothering me:

Just for Fun

When you are a competitor, you always find a way.

> International Harvester couldn't get steel to its factory in Melrose Park, Illinois, because of a truck drivers' union strike. The company couldn't use nonunion labor because of snipers on the freeway. Finally, the company rented school buses and dressed drivers as nuns, loaded the buses with steel, and made the deliveries. No one would shoot at school buses driven by nuns, right?[14]

Game on.

Chapter 4

Decide to Set Goals

*"A person should set his goals as early as he can and devote
all his energy and talent to getting there. With enough
effort, he may achieve it. Or he may find something
that is even more rewarding. But in the end, no matter
what the outcome, he will know he has been alive."*

—Walt Disney[1]

An elderly carpenter was ready to retire and told his employer of his
plans to leave the house-building business and enjoy his extended
family. The contractor was sorry to see his good worker go and asked
if he could build just one more house as a personal favor.

The carpenter said yes, but in time it was easy to see that his heart
wasn't in his work. His workmanship was shoddy and he used infe-
rior materials. It was an unfortunate way to end a dedicated career.
When the carpenter finished his work, the employer came to inspect
the house and handed the front-door key to the carpenter. "This is your
house," he said, "my gift to you."

The carpenter was shocked. If only he had known he was building
his own house, he would have done it all so differently.[2]

Psalm 90:12 states, "Teach us to number our days aright, that we may
gain a heart of wisdom." Goals help us "number our days" and determine what is next in our lives. This chapter will relieve the pressure of
having to know the future to set goals and inspire you to simply focus on
doing what is obvious to move the adventure on your heart forward.

Most of us have good intentions. But life is demanding, and we are
flooded with options and decisions that can easily distract us from living out those good intentions. The two processes that help make our

intentions a reality are *priorities* and *goal setting*. Robert J. McKain says, "Set priorities for your goals. A major part of successful living lies in the ability to put first things first. Indeed, the reason most major goals are not achieved is that we spend our time doing second things first."[3]

What Are Priorities?

Establishing priorities is the process of determining what comes before. There are too many choices in life to say yes to all of them, so we must have a system for determining what comes before other things in importance. This is a prerequisite for setting goals because we cannot decide what we will focus on until we determine what really matters to us.

Priorities are a great friend. They give us focus, higher energy, more confidence in our decisions, and more stability in our emotions. One of the great benefits of identifying our priorities is knowing what to say no to.

If you have any talent at all, you will be asked to do things for other people. Once word gets out that you are willing to assist, you will be asked over and over again. You don't want to disappoint people, but you also don't want to give your life away to things that are trivial to you. Priorities help you clearly identify the pursuits that warrant your attention and which ones are best left to other people.

What Are Your Priorities?

To help you determine what your priorities are, fill out the list below. Rank each item with an *A, B,* or *C.* If you rank something as an *A,* that means it's very important to you. You would keep your *A* activities even if that meant you couldn't do an item ranked *B* or *C.* A *B* ranking means it's not a main focus, but it's still important and you don't feel like it can go undone. A *C* means if it gets done fine, but if it doesn't, no sweat. *Cs* are those things you can drop when things get hectic or the quality can suffer a bit and it doesn't make you crazy.

___ being in good physical shape

___ having a neat, clean room/house

___ close friendships

___ being popular

___ having fun as a family (trips, vacations, kick-around time)

___ succeeding in your career/school

___ developing your talents to their fullest

___ doing fun things (movies, shopping, video games)

___ earning money

___ being involved in your local church

___ being involved in community activities (community theater, clubs, sports)

___ having a nice car

___ furthering your education

___ sending and receiving emails

___ achieving financial success

___ social networking (Facebook, Twitter, blogs)

___ having stylish/trendy clothes

___ spending time alone

___ spending time on a hobby

After you fill out this list, show it to the people who know you best. Ask them to look it over for two reasons. First, you want them to be aware of what is important to you so they understand a little better why you do what you do. Second, ask them to add anything to the list they are aware of that you may have missed because "many advisers make victory sure" (Proverbs 11:14).

Before I went through this exercise I would have given you the standard priority answer. The most important thing in my life is my relationship with God. Second is my wife, followed by my family. After that comes my career and my ministry, followed by my personal desires. This reflects part of what is important to me, but after going through this list, I realized that what is important to me is not as simple as a few things I can rank A, B, C, etc.

For instance, I realized that I am sharper mentally, spiritually, and emotionally when I consistently work out. I grew up playing sports and found athletic activities to be an effective escape from some of the stressful dynamics of my home growing up. For me, exercise is a safe place as well as a competitive pursuit. I realized working out is an *A* that makes everything else in my life better when I keep it active and in balance. I also realized that I need part of my life clean and highly organized or I lose focus. This is a challenge because I have a rather creative family. My wife and kids all value creative pursuits and spontaneous opportunities, which means they don't highly value things being in the same place every time.

Now, I don't want to be miserable to live with, but I need part of my life to be in order. As a result, I've made a deal with my family. The first part of the deal is that my garage is my garage. I have my tools in order with pegboard for the tools I use most often. My boys have permission to use the garage as long as they put things away when they're finished. If they violate the agreement, they are banished from the garage.

The second part of the deal is the living room. Everyone in my family knows that if they leave anything on the floor in the living room, I have permission to put it anywhere I want to. Sometimes I move their stuff to their rooms and sometimes I move their stuff to the shed. Once I even gathered up all the stuff in trash bags. I told them, "You have three days to decide what you want to keep from the bags in the garage. Anything that's not put away on the third day will be given away." They didn't really believe I would follow through. I hope somebody is enjoying the shoes and the basketball.

It's Your Turn

What did you discover that is really important to you that is not on the typical list of priorities?

Make It Your Goal to Set Goals

Goal setting is a skill anyone can learn. We tend to think of goal setting as a business activity reserved for those who want to be successful overachievers. This is just not the case. Goal setting is for every man. In my experience, the excuses men use for avoiding setting goals include:

- It is not possible to see the future so I'm just going to take what today gives me.
- I don't think we should try to plan out our whole lives. That's God's job.
- I think it's presumptuous to set goals. It feels like I'm telling God what to do.
- It gives me a headache.
- I don't need to set goals. My wife will tell me what to do.
- I'm not a leader at work. My boss sets the goals we all pursue.

In contrast to these opt outs, Proverbs 16:9 declares, "In his heart a man plans his course." It is part of being human to make plans about where we're heading. The reason we can all do this is that goal setting is simply the process of choosing what comes next. We are all headed in some direction. That direction is either deliberate or accidental. You don't have to know what will happen five years from now or even five days from now. Your job is to figure out what's next, and then pursue it with all your heart.

In this pursuit, God is an active partner. The second half of Proverbs 16:9 states, "but the LORD determines his steps." As we pursue what's next in our lives, Jesus guides our steps in the direction that's best for us. If we are not moving, the direction we receive is, "Get moving. Search your heart and choose a course, then I will determine your steps." We can do this with great confidence because God is fully invested in our lives. The principle is repeated in Proverbs 19:21, "Many are the plans in a man's heart, but it is the LORD's purpose that prevails." We are free to make plans because God created us that way, and He has promised that His purpose will prevail.

I can tell you with full confidence that God has a plan for your life. He created you at this time in history because it is your place. He created you with gifts and talents because He has a mission to accomplish through you. He can't explain His whole plan to you at once because it's too big and too complicated for you to grasp in one sitting. He unfolds His plan for you one step at a time. As the goal becomes clear, you gain confidence to make commitments. As you head for that goal, you grow as a man. When you get close to that goal, a new direction will unfold that will take you to the next step in His plan for your life. This script will be played out over and over as God leads you on your adventure. We engage in the process by setting goals that help us identify what is next.

When I was a sophomore in college, I sensed in a strong way God's call to ministry. I was discipling two of my peers and loving it. I said to myself one day, *I want to do this for the rest of my life.* I therefore set a goal: "I am going to join the staff of Campus Crusade for Christ when I graduate and work with college students as a campus staff member." I was convinced this was God's plan for my life, so I began to attend training conferences with this ministry. It was at these conferences that I developed a relationship with my wife, Pam. When we married before our junior year, I assumed we would both join Campus Crusade staff after we graduated. Then the ministry on our campus was removed.

Those of us who were active in this ministry decided to attend the same church and see if we could develop something similar with the church's youth group. This was my introduction to church ministry, and I fell in love with what was happening. I saw teenagers make significant decisions as they found their stride. I, therefore, set a new goal for my life: "I want to become a youth pastor. I am going to work with teenagers until I'm 40, and then I will reevaluate."

I focused on finishing my education, and then landed a job at that same church working with junior high, high school, and college students. The ministry grew, and many of those students have become effective leaders in their churches. After eight years of youth ministry, however, I noticed my prayers were changing. I began to talk to God about all the aspects of the church, from the worship services to men's ministry to leadership training to children's ministry. One day as I was praying, a distinct thought crossed my mind: *Put up or shut up. Bill, if you think you know how to run a church, then go run a church.* Whoa, I was stunned. So I set a new goal: "I want to be a preaching pastor for an indefinite period of time."

In 1988, I moved my family to San Diego to pastor a church where I preached, pastored, and led for fifteen years. Two years into that venture, I asked Jim Conway to mentor me so that I would avoid making mistakes of inexperience. After meeting with him for two years, he said one day, "Sally and I would like to coauthor a book with you and Pam, if you're willing." I had no thought of being a writer. It had never occurred to me, never entered my imagination, never been part of my prayers, and it had never been a dream of mine. When Jim said it, however, I knew immediately it was part of God's plan for me, so I set a new goal: "I will write this book with Jim and Sally and see what happens."

Well, the book came out in 1994 and we got a phone call one day.

"Hello, is this Bill Farrel?"

"Yes it is."

"The Bill of Bill and Pam Farrel?"

"Yes it is."

"Do you two speak at marriage conferences? Our church is planning a weekend retreat, and we're looking for a couple to speak. Do you do that?"

Pam and I looked at each other, and I responded, "Sure, we do that." We had never talked about doing this or dreamed it would be part of our ministry, but the opportunity was clear, so we set a new goal: "We will pursue a part-time speaking ministry while I pastor this church so we can extend our ministry to more people."

I assumed this would be my rhythm for the rest of my career, and it appeared that way for 14 years. Then in 2007, we interviewed twice on Focus on the Family and released a video curriculum with LifeWay Christian Resources. The requests for speaking began to pour in. We had a decision to make, and I set a new goal: "We will pursue a speaking and writing ministry full-time in an attempt to help as many people as possible grow in their most important relationships." I would never have recognized this as God's plan earlier in my life, but as it unfolded, each step was so clear it was impossible to miss. This is what goals in partnership with God do for you. As you do what's next, God's purpose prevails.

Take a STEP

Learning to do what is next rescues you from living an accidental life, which appears to be the way most men live. They react to what happens, then react to what happens, then react again without any thought of what direction they ought to be going. When you live this way, things may accidentally turn out okay, but most likely the accidental results of your life will not please you.

The simplest way I know to get started with goal setting is to develop the habit of taking a STEP. Four vital areas will help guide your life if you consistently look out for what's next in each of these pursuits. These four areas are your:

- **S**piritual growth
- **T**eam
- **E**nergy
- **P**roductivity

Your Spiritual Growth

If you know Jesus as your personal Savior, your body is a temple of the Holy Spirit (1 Corinthians 6:19). He lives within you, and His power is available to help you with challenges, empower you for relationships, and provide much needed wisdom for decisions. This is a power worth harnessing, and it is contained in a relationship that can be fostered. When you set a goal of what you want to do next to grow spiritually, you set yourself up to benefit from what God has to give you.

The place to start is with the spiritual disciplines. Consider the following questions in setting a goal for your spiritual growth.

- What would you like to read next in the Bible?
- What would you like to study next in the Bible?
- How do you want to grow in the area of prayer?
- Do you want to fast over any decision coming up in your life?
- Is there a sermon series you want to listen to?

Once you've considered the typical disciplines, you may want to consider nonconventional methods that work for you. Some men like to hike and pray. Others like to work out and pray. Some men like to take personal retreats where they get away from everyone and everything to spend time alone with God. Still others journal to focus their thoughts. You may want to set a goal for an activity that does not fit into the typical disciplines but that will help you connect with Jesus.

Two spiritual activities are especially helpful to me. The first is the habit of asking Jesus to lead in prayer. I like to find a quiet place and say to Him, "Okay, You go first." I then assume any thought that comes to mind is something He wants me to pray about. I don't worry about whether the thoughts are positive or negative, good or bad. I simply assume He knows best and trust Him to bring up the most important topics for conversation. I will keep this process going until my mind goes quiet. At that time, I either add my own requests or simply wrap it up for that day.

The other activity is listening to sermons or Christian music while I work in the yard. There's something about getting my hands dirty while I fill my mind with truth that helps me get closer to Jesus and gain clarity in my life. I have not found these two mentioned in typical discussions of spiritual disciplines, but they help clear my thinking and give direction to my spiritual growth.

Your Team

Some people in your life are vital to your success and well-being. These relationships need extra attention and deliberate effort. You need to spend time with these people, plan activities with them, and look for ways to connect with them in order for these relationships to flourish. Here are some areas of your personal team you may want to work on:

FAMILY

- How much time do I want spend talking with each family member?
- What do I want to do together with my family this year?
- Do I ask questions about what/how they are doing?

- Do I show respect for each family member?
- Do I know how to motivate each member of my family?

FRIENDS

- Do I look out for their best interests?
- Do I encourage and support them?
- Am I choosing friends who look out for my best interests?
- Do I have a plan for staying connected with them?
- Do I give and take in activities we do together?

MENTOR(S)

A mentor is "a wise and trusted counselor or teacher."[4] The best mentor is:

- Someone who is good at what you want to be good at
- Someone who is older than you
- Someone you are comfortable with
- Someone who has experienced more of life than you
- Someone living a healthy and productive life
- Someone you would consider a role model
- Someone you trust to steer you in the right direction if you are getting off track
- Someone you are willing to be accountable to
- Someone you can be honest with whether you're messing up or doing well
- Someone you can confide in

Do you have a mentor in your life? If not, you may want to choose a man you trust to help you move forward in a specific area of life. You most likely will have many mentors in your lifetime. You don't necessarily need another dad, but there are men around you who can help you make progress faster than you could make on your own.

Your Energy

Everything you do requires energy. If you have more energy than necessary for your responsibilities, you will conclude that life is relatively easy and stress will be low. If your responsibilities overwhelm your energy level, you will feel exhausted as stress surrounds you like a heavy fog. You can't make your responsibilities just go away, so it is vital that you deliberately do what keeps your energy level as high as possible. To maintain a high level of energy, you must invest in the areas of life that are important to you, such as:

- Your education
- Emotional well-being
- Health
- Social life
- Your finances
- Other _____

Activities that may be vital to you may include:

- Hobbies
- Sports
- Reading
- Computer time
- Watching TV
- Listening to music
- Going to the mall
- Going to the beach
- Other _____

For me, the two areas that add energy to my life are working out and reading novels. When I keep these two activates consistent in my life, I usually have enough energy for everything else that I need to do. When I neglect these two, the rest of life just seems harder. Therefore, it makes sense for me to always have a goal of what I'm going to do next in my exercise routine and my casual reading schedule. For you it may be a commitment to any of the following activities:

- Eat regularly
- Sleep eight hours per night
- Talk daily with certain friends
- Have an exercise routine
- Play in competitive sports
- Practice a musical instrument
- Other _____

Your Productivity

This is what most of us think about when we consider goals. Each of us has been called to make a living, support our families, and make a productive contribution to life. As a result, it is wise to consider what you will do next in your career, your education, and your influence on others.

- If you are in school, what grades do you want to get this semester?
- What type of work do you want to pursue?
- What position do you want to attain in that field?
- What type of advancement do you want to pursue in your career?
- Who are the people you would like to personally influence?
- How would you like to use your talent, time, and treasures in your community?

We have all had a stark reminder with the crash of Tiger Woods of why it's important to balance our goals in all four areas. His career accomplishments are legendary, and he will probably go down in history as the greatest golfer of all time. His endorsements were impressive and have set him up financially for life. His personal life, however, turned out to be a disaster. After tens of thousands of dollars spent on illicit sex, he has lost the respect of the public, severely damaged his marriage, greatly complicated his relationship with his kids, and alienated most of his sponsors. After all the great things he accomplished, the words most people will probably remember about him were spoken by Swedish golfer Jesper Parnevik, the man who introduced him to his wife: "We thought he was a better guy than he is."[5] If Tiger had been as deliberate with his personal life as he was with his career, we would probably still be admiring him.

Getting Started

Phil McGraw gives great advice when it comes to goals: "Know your goal, make a plan and pull the trigger."[6] For most people it's best to focus on one goal in each area. Any progress you make will help produce a habit of growth. This habit of growth will strengthen other areas of your life as well. Therefore, any area you work on will cause personal growth that will affect more than the one goal you chose.

If this is your first experience with goal setting, you may want to start out small and more short-term because short-range goals are easier to reach. When you begin to see results, your motivation will escalate and you'll be ready to add your longer-term goals. In time, goal setting will become a regular part of your life. Ralph Waldo Emerson said, "That which you persist in doing becomes easier to do. Not that the nature of the thing itself has changed, but that your ability to do it has increased."[7] To establish goal setting as a consistent habit, set up a strategy.

Choose goals based on your priorities. Refer back to your "What Is Important to Me" list (see pp. 66–67) when you set goals. Ask yourself, "Are my goals helping me accomplish the most important things in my life?" It does you no good to set goals in areas of life you don't especially care about. You may convince yourself these are important, but you will have no passion or drive to do anything with them. Energize the aggressiveness God placed in your soul and spend your best efforts on your best pursuits.

Be specific when you choose goals. Goals work best when you can evaluate them. If they are too vague or too general, you cannot tell when you've made progress. The most effective goals are specific. Choosing to read one chapter in Matthew and one chapter in Proverbs each day is better than saying, "I want to read the Bible more this month." Saying, "I will spend one hour every Tuesday night talking with my wife about any subject she wants to discuss," is better than saying, "I need to be more patient with my wife when she talks." Choosing to work out for 30 minutes each morning before I go to work is better than saying, "I need to get in shape." Vague statements communicate good intentions, but they do little to produce the action that makes a difference. A specific commitment to specific goals is a powerful force in creating real change in our lives.

Organize your life to accomplish these goals. Don't settle for goals that are just words on paper. Give them feet and let them run. Periodically ask yourself if you are strategically putting time and effort into the right things in order to reach your goals without getting sidetracked. Each night before you go to bed, take a couple of minutes to review your goals and ask, "What can I do tomorrow that will help me do what is next in my life?" Once a month, review your progress by asking, "What progress have I made this month? What can I do to reward myself for the progress I have made?"

Commit yourself wholeheartedly to these goals. Often it takes hard work to reach your goals. You need to be willing to do what it takes. Sometimes it means being willing to sacrifice other things when working toward a goal. You will be tired, you will strain yourself intellectually, physically, emotionally, and spiritually, but you will be fulfilled as you realize it's worth the effort.

Adjust your goals when it is obvious to do so. Sometimes situations occur that will cause you to reevaluate your goals. It's okay to change them as you need to because they are *your* goals. Life changes as God leads you in the path of His will. Remember, He gives you what you need next and usually does not give you the whole plan at once. A big part of goal setting includes elimination and recommitment. You may reach one goal only to find that it has led you to a new and different goal. Don't let that discourage you. Through this process you learn valuable lessons that prepare you for the next season of your adventure.

It's Your Turn

The next STEP I'm going to take in my life is:

My Spiritual Growth:

Areas of spiritual growth you may want to work on (choose one):

☐ Bible reading

☐ Bible study

☐ Bible memorization

☐ Prayer

☐ Seminars/retreats

☐ Media (podcast, radio, video, TV)

☐ Church attendance

☐ Books to read

☐ Small group attendance

My Team:

Areas of your personal team you may want to work on:

☐ Goals with my spouse/family

Time together (daily, weekly, monthly, quarterly, vacations)

Training (seminars/retreats, books, personal counseling, classes)

☐ Goals with my mentors

Do I need to find one?

Area of life to focus on:

Candidates:

☐ Goals with my friends

Time together (daily, weekly, monthly, quarterly)

Activities:

My Energy:

Ways to maintain energy that you may want to consider:

Personal growth
☐ Seminars/retreats
☐ Books
☐ Personal counseling
☐ Classes/online or media-driven growth
☐ Small groups
☐ Hobbies
☐ Health

My Productivity:

To determine what productivity goal you would like to set, consider these questions:

What do you want to accomplish next in your career?

What do you want to accomplish next in your ministry?

Who do you want to influence next?

Career Goal (advancement, financial goal, build new relationships)

Ministry Goal (give more time, give less time, find a new ministry, train for leadership, help someone else do what you do)

Get in the habit of setting goals today so you will never have to say, "If only I had known I was building my own house, I would have done it differently."

Just for Fun

Sometimes strategic plans get lost in translation.

A blonde woman was terribly overweight, so her doctor put her on a diet. "I want you to eat regularly for two days, then skip a day, and repeat this procedure for two weeks. The next time I see you, you'll have lost at least five pounds."

When the woman returned, she'd lost nearly twenty pounds.

"Why, that's amazing," the doctor said. "Did you follow my instructions?"

She nodded. "I'll tell you, though, I thought I was going to drop dead that third day."

"From hunger, you mean?" the doctor asked.

"No, from skipping."[8]

Chapter 5

Decide to Be Busy

"Inaction breeds doubt and fear. Action breeds confidence and courage. If you want to conquer fear, do not sit home and think about it. Go out and get busy."

—Dale Carnegie[1]

After his junior season playing high school football, my youngest son, Caleb, shared his dream with me. "I want to play college football. I would love to compete at a Division I school, but I'd be okay with Division I-AA or II. I just want to play."

I was impressed with his desire and apparent focus. Day after day he would talk. Day after day he would dream. And day after day he would sit at home doing nothing about it.

I finally had heard enough talk. I interrupted him one day and said, "Caleb, I think you have an awesome goal here, but you're not working nearly hard enough to get there. If you want to play college ball, you've got to get in the weight room at least four days a week. You have to run more, do more drills, and get stronger. College is not like high school. It takes a lot more dedication and skill. So, either get busy preparing yourself for college athletics or stop talking about it."

He just stared at me with that look that said, "I've been exposed." He didn't explain himself or argue with me. He just walked out of my home office and got busy. He took the challenge seriously, committed to a diligent workout program, and had an excellent senior season. As I'm writing this book, he's preparing for his sophomore season in college. He made it because he got busy.

Run at Your Pace

It's impossible to be a decisive man and not be busy. I'm not talking about the kind of busy that has you looking to speed up your life every year just because there's more and more to do. I mean the kind of purposeful busy that leads to a productive, effective life. So how do you figure out how busy you should be? How do you find the balance between underachieving and burning out?

It begins with finding your pace. Every man has a pace at which he functions best, and he can be highly effective if he will commit to live at his pace. I like to think of the following five metaphors to describe the possibilities for the speed at which a man can live: the Muscle Car, the Sports Car, the Semi, the Mail Truck, and the Tractor.

The Muscle Car

Muscle cars depict the man who likes to go fast and stay focused. He likes to charge hard and is always looking for a reason to step on the gas pedal. He loves quick decisions, big opportunities, and is happiest when he has something on the schedule that demands his attention and requires his best effort. He easily grows restless and can often be heard to say, "Let's go." He would rather try something that might fail than sit around thinking too hard about what might happen.

Muscle car men tend to be epic. They have probably experienced monumental success, and they have most likely failed in dramatic fashion because they are always doing something big. Their greatest asset is they don't look to the left or the right. They stay focused on the goal with clarity and commitment. They experience little fear because the direction of their life is clear, unhindered, and uncomplicated.

I've had the privilege of knowing a few of these men in my journey. David Jeremiah is definitely a muscle car. I had the benefit of being on staff at Shadow Mountain Community Church for three years under his leadership, and he asked me to do a research project to determine what would help our small group ministry grow. After interviewing many at the church and then talking with similar ministries, I concluded that a sermon-based small group ministry was exactly what this church needed. Dr. Jeremiah is one of the most talented, most influential Bible teachers in the world today, so it made sense to me that small groups at the church he pastors would work best if they followed his teaching. After reviewing the plan, he asked me, "Would you run it?"

Observing his leadership style was a fascinating education. Shadow Mountain Ministries enjoys amazing influence. It begins with a church that averages 5000 people in attendance every weekend and supports world missions with 20 percent of every dollar donated. It includes two elementary schools, a junior high school, and a high school. On the same campus is San Diego Christian College and Southern California Seminary. In addition to all this, Turning Point Ministries broadcasts Dr. Jeremiah's sermons on 1300 radio stations in addition to weekly television broadcasts that cover the United States, Canada, the United Kingdom, Europe, Australia, and New Zealand.

I will never forget the day he announced in a church service, "I know what our project as a church is supposed to be this year. We are going to deliver a Bible to every home in our city in one day. The money has already been donated for printing the Bibles. To accomplish this task, we need 1500 people to show up on one Saturday to make the deliveries. If you would like to be one of these 1500, you can sign up this morning." He stomped on the gas that day, and we pulled it off. Every home in our city was presented a copy of God's Word, and the stories of people who were welcomed, rejected, encouraged, and strengthened were told for months.

Another one of my muscle car friends is John. He has been extremely successful in the financial world. He told me one day, "What I know how to do is make money. I don't have the patience to sit and listen to people, so I'd rather support ministries with money and help the gifted ministers do their job."

Two experiences have focused John's big thinking. First, he discovered a relationship with Jesus Christ that has given him a stable foundation for his strength. Second, he lost two brothers to drug addiction. His brothers were talented and big-hearted young men who got lost in the drug world and had their hopes and dreams extinguished long before their time. John loved his brothers and was determined that their deaths would not be in vain. To honor their memory and inspire others to find a great life without drugs, he founded the Sundt Memorial Foundation. The main focus of the foundation is the Natural High DVD series, which features testimonials from stars and peers that challenge teenagers to find their own natural high that is drug free. The foundation has produced four different DVDs, and the goal is to give a DVD to every school in America. The latest, *Natural High 4*, was sent to over 90,000 schools in September 2009, and educators have committed to show this inspiring message to 1.1 million students.[2] John only knows how to do things big, and the world is better for it.

If you are a muscle car kind of man, you will live at a faster pace and pursue bigger goals than most. You may, however, be impatient with others who move slower and with greater caution. Others point out to you the dangers ahead, but you will minimize the obstacles because you are used to charging ahead to success. You will benefit by listening to advisors who approach life differently than you, but you will always end up going fast.

The Sports Car

Some of you move more like sports cars. These vehicles are fun and agile, and they prefer roads that have lots of turns and quick transitions. The surprise around the next corner is what you live for. New opportunities, new experiences, and new discoveries keep life interesting. Without these spontaneous enhancements, life for you becomes boring and frustrating. Unlike the muscle car, you do not want to just go fast in one direction. You love variety and epiphanies. Your interest in new possibilities causes you to run almost as fast as the muscle car but on a much different road.

My friend Steve runs at a sports car pace. He is unpredictable, spontaneous, and always in motion. He's one of the most inspirational men I know and has an uncanny ability to get people to do things they wouldn't ordinarily do. I love hanging around Steve because we just have so much fun.

He and I once led a bicycle trip with around 50 high school students along the central coast of California. We had ridden most of the day, and we were all comfortably settling into the church where we had arranged housing. Suddenly, Steve blurted out, "Everyone grab your blankets and sleeping bags and get on the bus."

"What are we going to do?" a couple of us asked him.

"We're going to have fun. Let's go."

Then he headed for the bus. Without details and without explanation, we all grabbed sleeping bags and blankets and got on board. The bus drove to the beach, and we all piled out to watch the sunset.

At least, that was the plan. But the wind was blowing and it was cold. We couldn't just sit on the beach to watch the sun go down because sand was blowing in our eyes. We all found ourselves hiding behind small dunes, wrapped in sleep gear, peeking out every once in a while to catch a glimpse of the sun. It was miserable and marvelous all at the same time. No cautious person would have come up with the idea. No methodical man would have called us to action. Steve took a quick turn, and we are still talking about it as a great memory.

It's inspiring to follow a sports car. Steve has been a successful youth pastor and an effective coach, and his adventurous heart has even led him and his wife to missions work in several countries on the State Department's "Most Dangerous Countries" list. They also adopted a child from one of those countries. Teenagers for 30 years have been thanking him for his influence on their lives as they discovered potential within themselves they never imagined they had.

At other times, it's irritating to follow a sports car. Steve regularly runs out of gas. He changes plans without consulting others who are affected. He fails to explain himself because even he isn't sure what's around the next corner. We've all tried to slow him down, but we found we didn't really like him as much when he wasn't skidding around corners and finding new adventures.

The Semi

Some men operate more like a semitruck. They start and stop slow. Course corrections must be planned out, and they take time to navigate. Once semis get moving, they travel long distances at consistent speeds without a lot of variation. Their pace is steady and even. They don't move as fast as muscle cars and sports cars, but they can carry large amounts of responsibility, and they faithfully plod along until the work is done. They're not spectacular and they're not nimble, but they keep the rest of us going. These men are the backbone of our communities, our organizations, and our churches.

My friend Peter is one of these men. He has worked as an accountant, controller, and is now the CFO of his company. He loves the back office and has no desire to be on stage or up front. He shows up to work on time every day. He works long hours when necessary but never seems stressed by the job. He smiles when he greets you and never seems to be in a hurry even though he has piles of work on his desk. He meets deadlines with skill and produces reports that are easy to understand and simple, even though they reflect a complex collection of information.

I can't think of anything specific that Peter has ever said, but my respect for him is sky high. He is not spectacular, and he doesn't demand to be noticed. He is, however, reliable, consistent, easy to be around, and steady. I always know what to expect when I'm with him. I'm also amazed at how much he accomplishes every week, even though it doesn't look as if he's working hard, and he always seems to be able to stop and talk when I stop by his office. He just does the right thing, in the right way, so he is reliable, trustworthy, and steady.

The Mail Truck

This man has a sign on his back, "Makes Frequent Stops." He is intensely interested in people and finds his life consistently interrupted by conversations and projects to help others. Everyone loves to see him coming because he makes them feel important. He is engaging and encouraging. He starts with energy and then stops to help. He makes enthusiastic commitments, then stalls because of the needs of someone close to him. He eventually gets back on task but justifies the delay because he helped people along the path.

Lest you think this style is a bad thing, it appears to be the pace Jesus operated at often. It would be unfair to limit the Savior to just one pace, but this one is obvious. In John 4, "tired as he was from the journey [through Samaria], he sat down by the well" (v. 6). It was here that He engaged the woman from Samaria in the most significant conversation of her life. In John 5, Jesus is in Jerusalem celebrating one of the feasts of the Jews when He encountered a man who "had been an invalid for thirty-eight years" (v. 5). He interrupted His activities to heal this man. Sometime later, "as he went along, he saw a man blind from birth"

(John 9:1). He took time to give this man sight, which intensified His discussion with the other religious leaders of His day.

The Tractor

Tractors are incredibly useful, but they are slow. If you try to drive a tractor too fast, it makes a mess of things. Tractors plow the ground, dig furrows, plant seeds, and harvest crops. They move snow, move dirt, move rocks, and move farmers. Tractors don't make sharp turns, and they don't get speeding tickets. They take time off when the weather is bad, and they sit in barns until they are needed. They tend to have one speed, and they work at that speed all day. We take them for granted, but they do some of the most important work on earth.

My dad is a tractor. He's the most naturally content man that I know. He worked in the aerospace industry as a mechanical engineer, and he went to work at the same time every day and came home from work at the same time every day. He never remodeled his house. He never modified a car. He never had any great dreams for himself. He just calmly did his work. You would never know talking with him that he helped put men on the moon.

When it was time to relax, he could sit for long periods of time and just watch television. When he had a stroke at 48 years old, he settled into a life with diminished opportunities without complaint. He retired at 65 and joined the world of remote-control aircraft. He built planes, helped out with competitions, and served on the board of the local club. When his eyesight failed him at 67, he took that in stride and has been content to spend most of his time on his computer.

He is one of the most intelligent men I know, and I am always amazed when I talk with him about current events. He has also been to me the best example of integrity as he tenaciously keeps his promises and commitments. He just doesn't make many promises or commitments because tractors don't move fast.

All I can say to you tractor-type men is that when 24 inches of snow were covering the parking lot of our condominium last Christmas, I wasn't looking for a muscle car, a sports car, a mail truck, or even a semi to help me out. I was looking for a tractor.

It's Your Turn

Which of the five vehicles best represents the pace at which you like to live? Be bold in your assessment. You were created this way because it is part of God's plan for your life.

- The Muscle Car
- The Sports Car
- The Semi
- The Mail Truck
- The Tractor

What adjustments do you need to make to better enable you to live at this pace?

Find Your Threshold

Another reason why it's good to decide to be busy is that it helps you find your threshold of influence and effectiveness. To be sure, each of us has a unique potential, and we cannot all have the same level of productivity, influence, and authority. But all of us can probably accomplish more than we currently experience. If you could operate at your optimal pace every waking hour of every day, you would live the greatest possible life you are capable of.

None of us lives this way, however. If you are committed to find your pace and live at your speed, you will constantly make adjustments as you hover around your threshold. You will speed up in search of your pace. Then you'll probably exceed the speed that's best for you, which will cause stress and fatigue. In response, you'll slow down to recapture equilibrium. As you put the brakes on, you'll slow down too much, which will bring a sense of disappointment and also produce fatigue. Therefore, you'll speed up and start the cycle over again.

This search for the threshold of your effectiveness is the normal attitude of the apostle Paul. "I press on...straining toward what is ahead" (Philippians 3:12,13). "Just as you excel in everything...excel in this grace of giving" (2 Corinthians 8:7). "Excel still more" (1 Thessalonians 4:1 NASB). "Work out your salvation with fear and trembling" (Philippians 2:12). "I beat my body and make it my slave" (1 Corinthians

9:27). He wanted to know just how much he was capable of, and he wanted to live at the pace that was most effective. This is also how the most vibrant men live.

One of the valued treasures in my office is a football signed by members of the Washington Redskins team. Most notable are the names Darrell Green (defensive back and the fastest man in football for a while) and Ken Harvey (linebacker and four-time Pro Bowler). I met these men at a church in the Washington DC area where Pam and I spoke at two marriage conferences. Ken was our personal assistant making sure we had everything we needed and transporting us to our destinations.

The first thing I noticed about Ken was his impressive physical appearance. His arms were like sledge hammers, his shoulders were like mountaintops, and every muscle you could see rippled as he moved. He had a successful career and had invested his earnings well so he could, if he wanted, take it easy for the rest of his life. But this is not the kind of man Ken is.

On Saturday morning of the conference, Ken asked if we'd be willing to spend a little time with him later that day, which we were glad to do. When we got together, Ken said, "I wanted to talk with you because I have a passion to write children's stories, and I want you to help me evaluate if you think I can get published. I brought along a couple of the books I've been working on. Maybe you could take a look at them and give me some tips."

My first reaction was laughter. I just couldn't picture kids cuddling up in this strong man's lap as he read a story to them. My second reaction was admiration. Here was a man looking for his pace. He knew he couldn't just stop living. He had been a competitive athlete for years. He was used to being productive, busy, and focused. He knew how to follow his passion for a game he loved. He now realized he loved kids and he loved stories for kids, so why shouldn't he pursue his dream? He wasn't discontent with his life; he just wanted to keep going. He wanted to live all his years to the fullest, not just the 11 years he played in the NFL.

Rick is another friend I have great admiration for; he's a tractor who also lives a vibrant life. He's one of the most faithful men I know, even though he would never impress you when you first meet him. He and his wife raised two kids of their own, and then they sensed that God wanted them to get involved in foster care. They took care of a girl who looked as if she could be one of their own. They fell in love with her, so they adopted her. They then took on two girls who definitely did not look like their kids. Rick and his wife also fell in love with these girls, so they adopted them too. Finally, they took care of a young boy from a drug-addicted mom and fell in love with him. They now have more adopted children than they have natural children, and Rick loves them all the same. I would never have guessed that Rick had the energy, compassion, or drive to raise this many kids, but he kept looking for his threshold. It turns out it was much larger than I or anyone else who knows Rick thought.

Then there's Big John. When I was working as a small group pastor, I said to myself, *That man has a great heart. I bet he'd be a great small group leader.* I challenged him to start a group with a commitment to help him get started.

"I just don't know, Bill," he said. "I'll pray about it, but I never pictured myself doing anything like this."

I gave him a couple of weeks to think it over, and then I approached him again. Same response—"I'll keep praying, but I'm just not sure."

"I am sure, John," I told him. "I'm confident that you would be really good at this."

I knew this was something he should do, but I could tell his confidence was low. He was a painter and had been most of his adult life. He was confident working with his hands, but he didn't think he had any teaching, leading, or ministry skills. I just couldn't accept this about him. I was convinced he was supposed to do this, so I decided to keep pushing until he either started a group or told me to stop asking.

I don't know if he finally started a group to get me to stop pestering him or because he had a change of heart, but the beginning was remarkable. Thirteen men showed up for the first early morning gathering. They bonded quickly with John, and one man opened up unexpectedly at that first meeting. The men gathered around him and prayed for him.

John was amazed. He came straight to my office after the meeting and said, "You will not believe what just happened. A bunch of men actually showed up, and you should've seen what God did. This man opened up with some tough things. Instead of criticizing him or making fun of him, the other men just gathered around and prayed for him. Men don't even like to pray out loud, but they prayed for him. Thanks for pushing me to do this."

John hasn't missed a week since. The group has continued to grow so that John has consistent influence now in the lives of 25 men. Most of these men have pretty rough backgrounds, but they are finding hope, strength, wisdom, and focus as they grow together. They decided to name the group the Junkyard because they believe God took them all from the junk heap, rebuilt them, shined them up, and transformed them into men who can live strong lives. If you hang around John for long, you'll hear him say, "Hey, God doesn't make junk. Don't tell me He can't handle your life."

I love hanging around men who want to know where their threshold of energy, influence, and potential lies.

Make Time to Run at Your Pace

As my youngest son was making the transition from high school to college, I explained to him that his life was going to be less structured now, which made him more responsible for his schedule. I asked him to put together a schedule so he could identify how much time he thought he could work.

He came back to me and said, "Okay, Dad, I've looked at my schedule, and between school and football, I don't think I'm going to have much time for anything else."

"Go through it with me," I said. "How much time will school take?"

"Well, I have 12 units plus football."

I explained to him that college classes usually take three hours per week for every unit—one hour in class and two hours outside of class doing homework and research. "That means school will take about 36 hours per week. How much time do you think football will take every week?"

He thought about it and then said, "Between practice, workouts, and games I think I'll spend about 20 hours every week."

"That's good," I said. "What are you going to do with the other 100 hours?"

His eyebrows raised. "What do you mean?"

"Well, you have 168 hours every week to organize. You just told me how you're going to use 56 of those hours. That leaves you with 112 hours to work with. What do you want to do with all those hours?"

It was eye-opening for him as he began to realize he had more time available to him than he'd thought.

We all have 168 hours every week to work with. We don't get extra hours if we do well, and we don't have any hours taken away from us if we have a disappointing week. Every week of every month of every year of your life, you have 168 hours to organize. It doesn't make sense to waste any of these hours by letting them just slip away.

We have been entrusted with our time, and we get to decide how to invest this treasure. With this time, there are a number of activities we need to work in:

- *Sleep.* We all need to sleep, although we all differ in how much sleep we need. The average seems to be around seven hours per day for a healthy life.

- *Meal preparation and time to eat.* A healthy diet requires time to prepare. When you eat well, you feel better and have more energy. When you rush this too much, you eat food that makes you lethargic and slows you down.

- *Personal hygiene.* You can't have influence if people don't want to be around you.

- *Personal growth and development.* Life is getting bigger every year, so we need to grow every year.

- *Work.* Your career can easily take too much time, but it is your responsibility and privilege to see to it that your family is provided for.

- *Time with family and friends.* Your wife and kids need time with you. God placed you in their lives to help them grow and make good decisions. Your friendships also need time to flourish. These relationships are always hungry, so they will take as much time as you can give them. It's up to you to decide how much of your time you can invest in these vital relationships.

- *Community involvement.* Jesus said the path to greatness is through serving others. To maximize your legacy, you will want to have some involvement in your church, your kids' leagues, or other community groups.

- *Interruptions.* Life gets interrupted because it's filled with problems that need to be solved. Also, modern technology fills our lives with tools that create interruptions.

- *Chores, maintenance of home and other possessions.* Unfortunately, everything in your life deteriorates, grows weeds, gets dirty, and wears out.

- *Time to relax and recharge.* You are not a machine. You are a man who needs time off and a good meal to recharge your battery for the next round.

Get a System

If you want to organize your time, you need to find a system that works for you. There are many options on the market, but the effective ones all share some common traits. Good systems provide a way for you to write down your schedule. None of us has a good enough memory to carry all our commitments in our minds. Men have told me my whole life, "I don't need to write down my schedule. I have it right here," as they point to their foreheads. These men have either oversimplified their schedules so they are underachieving or they aren't good at keeping track of their time.

You may choose to keep track of your schedule on your computer or on your cell phone. You may choose to carry a calendar you can write on or you may simply carry a daily to-do list. You may purchase a predesigned program or you may choose to design a system of your own. Whatever you decide on, get a system that you will use.

Develop a Habit

Once you've chosen a system, develop a habit of checking in with your system regularly. To get started, mark off on your calendar the nonnegotiable parts of your schedule. For instance, if you work for a company that requires you to be present during certain hours, this is nonnegotiable. You must show up on time (or early), and you must stay until you are released. You may also have set mealtimes with your family or a school schedule or a practice schedule for sports or music. Get these written down before you handle the creative options you have with your activities so you develop a habit of keeping routine things routine.

Choose a time each week to plan your schedule for the week ahead. It may be Sunday afternoon, Wednesday night, Saturday morning, or some other time of the week. The purpose of this time is to take a bird's-eye view of your week. Write in the specific meetings and commitments you know about. Doing this weekly makes time management a simple habit so that you don't have to spend undue energy trying to stay organized.

Finally, choose a time every day to review your schedule for the next day. If you do this daily, it should take only a few minutes. You will quickly get this time back the next day as you operate more efficiently.

It's Your Turn

Before you can write down your schedule you'll need to allocate your time. Fill in the chart below with the time you need for each activity. In the open spaces, add activities that are specific to your life.

Activity	Time needed
Sleep	
Meal preparation and time to eat	
Personal hygiene	
Personal growth and development	
Work	
Time with family and friends	
Community involvement	

Activity	Time needed
Interruptions	
Chores, maintenance of home and other possessions	
Time to relax and recharge	
Total:	168 hours

Just for Fun

There are times when it's obvious that you need to be busy.

A clergyman was walking down a country lane and saw a young farmer struggling to load hay back onto a cart after it had fallen off.

"You look hot, my son," said the cleric. "Why don't you rest a moment, and I'll give you a hand."

"No thanks," said the young man. "My father wouldn't like it."

"Don't be silly," the minister said. "Everyone is entitled to a break. Come and have a drink of water."

Again the young man protested that his father would be upset. Losing his patience, the clergyman said, "Your father must be a real slave driver. Tell me where I can find him and I'll give him a piece of my mind."

"Well," replied the young farmer, "he's under the load of hay."[3]

Chapter 6

Decide to Be Better

"Failure is not fatal, but failure to change might be."
—John Wooden[1]

In our efforts to succeed, it's best to be honest about our need to get better. If you don't, you run the risk of doing things that don't match your age. Consider the reaction of employers as they read these statements on job applications:

- "I was wholly responsible for two failed financial institutions."
- "I have become completely paranoid, trusting completely no one and absolutely nothing."
- "My goal is to become a meteorologist. But since I possess no training in meteorology, I suppose I should try stocks."
- "I procrastinate, especially when the task is unpleasant."
- "Instrumental in ruining entire operation for a Midwest chain store."
- "Please don't misconstrue my 14 jobs as job-hopping. I have never quit a job."
- "Reason for leaving last job: They insisted that all employees get to work by 8:45 a.m. every morning. I could not work under these conditions."
- "The company made me a scapegoat—just like my three previous employers."
- "References: none. I have left a path of destruction behind me."[2]

Needless to say, none of these people were hired.

You definitely don't want this to be your experience so "grow in the grace and knowledge of our Lord and Savior Jesus Christ" (2 Peter 3:18). This is the banner cry of a man's life. We don't need to be perfect and we don't need to be flawless. We just need to be better. We have been created to make progress each and every year. We are designed to grow in wisdom, in our skills, in our spiritual capacity, and in our decision-making ability. We are all flawed individuals with great potential, so improvement is always a possibility.

It is debatable whether Adam needed to grow before the fall. It is not debatable, however, whether he needed to grow after the fall. When we encounter him after he and Eve ate the fruit, he is hiding from God. Really, hiding from God? Who taught him that this was a good idea? What made him think this was even possible?

I became a grandfather in 2007, and I love to play with my granddaughter. Her name is Eden, so playing hide-and-seek with her is a reminder to me of the first hide-and-seek game played in the Garden of Eden. She will stand behind the kitchen trash can and pretend that she is hidden. She'll put a blanket over her head and act as though I can't see her. We laugh and scream with joy when she "comes out of hiding." This is an awesome game with a preschooler. It's not so awesome when a grown man plays this same game with God, but that's what Adam did.

Ever since Adam decided to rebel against God's clear directions, every person has been born with the need to grow (in addition to the need to experience God's forgiveness, but that's a topic for another time). Those who consistently grow experience some level of success in every season of their life. Those who fail to grow, however, will wake up one day and realize they are not ready for life's demands. These men tend to have spectacular moments early in life when their energy level is high and their inhibitions are low. As life matures, however, their skills are not sufficient for the challenge. Despite their best efforts, they lose opportunity, lose marriages, lose hope, or lose self-control as they get overwhelmed. Some of these men realize the need to grow and frantically try to catch up, but they find it to be almost impossible amidst the heavy demands of a family, career, and personal needs.

This does not have to be your story. It's impossible to ever be perfect during our days on earth, but each of us can be better a year from now than we are today. We can be better two years from now than we are a year from now. As you get better, life seems easier. It isn't that life has become less demanding or that you have been given a pass because of your effort. It's just that your skills are better developed to meet life's challenges.

The Laws of Personal Growth

So how does growth happen? How do you orchestrate life so that you are on a consistent path of improvement? The progress of personal growth is based on the application of four simple laws.

Growth Law 1: You will choose to listen to certain advice in your life. We live in a world of abundant information with limitless options for accessing advice. As you interact with this sea of knowledge, you will choose to filter input based on some philosophy of life. You may choose to randomly select information believing that you are the best judge of what is good for you to listen to. You may choose a mentor to help you filter information. It may be a formal mentor with whom you meet or a virtual mentor who has a presence in books or on the Internet. You may hang out in the blogosphere or among social networking sites where everyone has an opinion for public consumption. You may choose a religious leader or system to give direction to your life.

My advice for you is to filter everything you hear and read through the truth of the Bible. The Word of God is "God-breathed," which means God Himself passed on the information to human writers who recorded the truth using their distinct personalities. As a result, the principles of the Bible are true, reliable, and timeless.

Whatever you choose, you will listen to the advice of someone. If that advice is true, your life will be guided on a healthy, productive, and reliable path. If that advice is not true, your life will veer off in a manipulative, self-destructive, or distracting journey that will keep you from your potential and add turmoil to your daily existence. The advice you listen to forms the foundation of your life. Based on this advice, you will evaluate relationships, determine your career, form your attitudes, and make commitments.

It's amazing to me how many people never stop to consider whether the advice they listen to day after day is true, reliable, or worth following. Many people seem content to just follow the advice they are comfortable with, whether it's workable or not. Jesus' challenge to all men is to build your house on a rock that can withstand any storm rather than building on sand that will crumble and wash away when life gets rough (Luke 6:47-49).

Growth Law 2: You will make decisions based on this advice. The reason you collect advice is that you have decisions to make. Every day, you are confronted with hundreds of choices. Many of these are minor decisions, such as what to wear, what to eat, what type of toothpaste to use, what cell phone you carry. These are not life-changing choices, but they must be made regularly. Some of your decisions have far-reaching impact. Who will you marry? What career will you commit to? How will you raise your kids? What type of friends will you spend your time with? How will you vote? Where will you live? And the list goes on. Your life is filled with choices and every decision impacts your journey. That's why the saying, "You make your choices and your choices make you," should always be in focus.

This is where we give direction to the growth of our lives. Joshua 24 provides the clearest example I know of the need to decide based on the advice we choose to listen to.

> "Now fear the LORD and serve him with all faithfulness. Throw away the gods your forefathers worshiped beyond the River and in Egypt, and serve the LORD. But if serving the LORD seems undesirable to you, then *choose* for yourselves this day whom you will serve, whether the gods your forefathers served beyond the River, or the gods of the Amorites, in whose land you are living. But as for me and my household, we will serve the LORD" (vv. 14-15).

First, Joshua gives his advice: "Now fear the LORD and serve him with all faithfulness. Throw away the gods your forefathers worshiped beyond the River and in Egypt, and serve the LORD" (v. 14). Next, he challenges the people of Israel to make a choice: "But if serving the LORD seems undesirable to you, then *choose* for yourselves this day whom you will serve, whether the gods your forefathers served beyond the River, or the gods of the Amorites, in whose land you are living" (v. 15a). In essence, Joshua is saying, "You have heard what God has to say. You have also grown up under the advice of the Egyptians and the advice of your fathers who served other gods. It's now time for you to choose." Finally, Joshua publicly shares the decision he has made: "But as for me and my household, we will serve the LORD" (v. 15b). Joshua tells the rest of them, "I have evaluated the source of the advice that was available to me, and I have chosen to listen to God's truth and make decisions in my life based on what I learn from Him. Now it's your turn. What will you choose?"

This is where the cultural war impacts your life. We live in a world that is proud and longs to be self-sufficient. Men want to believe that they know best and are not in need of any outside input. This is why modern man has been on a crusade to push God out of daily life. With a vengeance, men have tried to prove we were not created and, therefore, not responsible to a Creator. With intense effort, men have legalized the killing of unborn babies as proof that we can set our own morality. With puffed out chests, we have declared that we are responsible for the destruction of our environment and we are powerful enough to rescue it. Without regard for future generations, we have run up the debt and redefined marriage to suit our quest to free ourselves from any eternal accountability. The only conclusion that can be reached is that men believe our lives are an accident and that everything is the result of random actions over time. Those who disagree are criticized and ridiculed.

As a result, the need to choose is becoming clearer with each passing year. You can either listen to random advice based on the limited perspective of other men or you can listen to the timeless truth authored by the Creator of life. If you listen to random advice, you will be embraced by modern society and applauded for your "tolerance." If you listen to timeless truth, you will be called weak, narrow-minded, and old fashioned. As for me and my house, we will serve the Lord because I am not willing to stake my eternal future on the random conclusions of fallible men.

Growth Law 3: Your decisions will influence your emotions, which either add to or drain energy from your pursuit. This is not a subject we like to talk about a lot as men, but the truth is that we are all emotional. Can you imagine what life would be like without your emotions? Can you imagine watching a funny movie without laughing, winning a competition without getting excited, or watching the birth of your child without being flooded with joy? Can you imagine never falling in love, never sensing the encouragement of a friend, or always talking in a monotone voice? Can you imagine being numb in every situation, never knowing fear or victory?

It would be miserable to be that kind of man. I'm not advocating for men to wear their emotions on their sleeve and constantly say, "I'm just telling you how I feel." I just want us to realize that God gave us emotional energy to fuel our lives and increase our effectiveness.

We harness our emotional power through decisions because our emotions follow our decisions. If you make healthy decisions that are compatible with the way God created life, you will have a positive emotional response to your opportunities, which will increase the energy you can utilize to pursue your dreams. If, on the other hand, you make decisions that are chaotic and contrary to God's ways, your emotions will grow chaotic and will eventually deplete the energy you could have spent on moving your dreams forward.

Growth Law 4: Your energy level determines the effectiveness of your efforts. The advice you listen to, the decisions you make, and the energy you have available influence you dramatically. When these are all lined up, pointing toward God's will for your life, your effectiveness grows exponentially. When, however, any of these three are pointed away from God's will, you will fight yourself to try to move forward. You will find growth is harder than it needs to be, life is more strenuous than it ought to be, and your effectiveness is less than it could be.

Emotions are like the engine that provides power to move your car forward, but it has no idea how to steer. Without the steering wheel and the brakes, the engine would lead to disaster every time. But without an engine, the brakes and the steering wheel are useless. Your decisions energize your emotional energy to get you moving. Truth effectively steers your life, and your discernment provides the braking that helps you move at the right speed at the right time to navigate the turns of your life. If any of these malfunctions, your entire life is affected.

Growth in Wisdom

Two vital areas of growth help us harness the potential of our lives. The first is *wisdom*. Wisdom is one of the most valuable possessions we will ever acquire during our adventure on earth.

> Wisdom is more precious than rubies,
>> and nothing you desire can compare with her.
>>> (Proverbs 8:11)

> "Whoever listens to me [wisdom] will live in safety
>> and be at ease, without fear of harm."
>>> (Proverbs 1:33)

> The fear of the LORD is the beginning of wisdom
>> all who follow his precepts have good understanding.
>> To him belongs eternal praise.
>>> (Psalm 111:10)

Since there is a beginning of wisdom, there must a progression in wisdom. We can grow in wisdom, insight, and understanding about life. So how do you set a plan to cause growth in your level of wisdom? In short, you build wisdom by asking questions. The more you learn about life, the more you realize you don't know much, which creates a need to learn more. One of the signs of maturity, therefore, is a commitment to ask questions.

The Question of Provision. The author of the book of James tells us, "If any of you lacks wisdom, he should ask God, who gives generously to all without finding fault, and it will be given to him" (James 1:5). The context of this promise confirms that those who seek to do God's will experience various trials along the path. These trials are like the difficulties of an athlete who feels pain, experiences setbacks, and strains his body as he seeks victory. Those who sit in the stands have many opinions about the game, but they are excused from the travails that go along with being a competitor.

James was writing to people who had given their hearts to Jesus. They had believed the gospel of Christ and had been born again through a vital encounter with the Holy Spirit. Their sins had been forgiven, they had received eternal life, and they had been delivered from judgment.

It would logically follow that God's blessing would be upon their lives. Instead, they were dispersed around the Roman Empire. Many of them were exiled from their homes, many of them lost their careers, and some lost loved ones because of their faith. They were surprised because life was harder than ever.

The logical question they were asking was, "Why?" "Why is this happening? Why now? Why is that person's life getting better while mine is getting worse? Why do I have to suffer after meeting my Savior?" The why questions are easy to come up with because life can be confusing from our limited perspectives. James's advice is, "Whenever you want to ask, 'Why?' ask for wisdom."

Whenever you ask God for wisdom, you can do so with great confidence because He gives it "generously to all without finding fault." God is generous with wisdom and has the habit of giving more than is necessary. He wants us to succeed and is willing to give us all the wisdom we need and a little extra to cause growth. He knows that we cannot process the answer to all of our why questions, so He promises to give us wisdom. We may not be able to understand why we are experiencing our current situation, but we can always know what the next step is that leads to growth and effectiveness.

"Without finding fault" means that God never complains when you ask for wisdom. He will never say to you, "You didn't do anything with the wisdom I gave you last time. Why should I give you more?" You will never hear Him proclaim, "This man used only 10 percent of the wisdom I delivered to him. Can anyone think of a reason I should give him more?" God never reacts in anger, disappointment, or frustration when we ask for wisdom. He simply says yes, and then gives us all we can handle.

The Question of Procedure. Wisdom is the ability to know how. When you are wise, you know how to apply truth to specific situations. When you are wise, you know how to handle conversations so that people leave the discussion with clear directions and elevated motivation. When you are wise, you know how to navigate through a project so that it gets done on time, on schedule, and on budget.

Wisdom, therefore, consistently asks, "How?" "How do I get this done? How should I approach this? How do I apply biblical principles to this situation?" In the Bible, enduring truth is presented in principles that can be applied to situations in our world rather than rules that have to be carried out in precise detail. In order to involve us as full participants, God has left much of the how of life up to us. Let me give a few examples to illustrate how this works:

Hebrews 11:24 says, "Let us consider how we may spur one another on to love and good deeds." The goal is clear. We are to figure out how to motivate one another so that love and good deeds characterize our lives. Others ought to be able to look at us and declare, "This man knows how to love, and this man does good to others." We are told to motivate one another, but we are not told how to do it. (See chapter 7, "Decide to Love.")

James 4:19 tells us to be "quick to listen, slow to speak and slow to get angry." In other words, we are supposed to be good listeners. We are supposed to talk less, and we are to guard against having an angry response because these interrupt listening. Again, the goal is clear. We are challenged to master the process of listening, but we are not told how to become a good listener.

Matthew 28:19 lays out God's purpose for us: "Make disciples of all nations." We know that disciples are disciplined followers, and we know that making disciples involves "baptizing them" and "teaching them to observe," but the method for accomplishing this is not spelled out. I believe it is because the method needs to adapt with each generation. Peter, James, and John could never have imagined the Internet with numerous online Bibles. Nathaniel, Matthew, and Andrew could never have imagined printed discipleship curriculum available in every known language. The goal has not changed, but we have methods at our disposal that previous generations would have thought impossible and future generations will consider old school.

Men who are seeking to grow in wisdom consistently ask, "How?" Men who are content to remain immature simply quote verses and hope that others can figure out for themselves how to live them out. They give directives without clear instructions and repeat them louder when they are not understood. They accuse others of being insubordinate or ignorant rather than admit they don't really know what they're doing.

When you find yourself in this bind, ask, "How?" God is more interested in your effectiveness than you are, but He is patient. He will wait until you ask with a sincere desire to learn. Please realize that you cannot manipulate God with any of these questions. You can't say to Him, "Okay, I'm playing by the rules. I'm asking so now You have to respond." He sees right through this and will use the opportunity to mold your heart so you become a more willing follower.

When you ask because you want to partner with Him to help others, the story changes. He longs for men who want to join with Him. He seeks those who are genuinely seeking Him. He has promised, "You will seek me and find me when you seek me with all your heart" (Jeremiah 29:13).

The Question of Perspective. Every action in our lives has a far-reaching, long-term reaction. "A man reaps what he sows" (Galatians 6:7). Wisdom has the ability to see down the road and recognize how today's decisions will affect tomorrow's circumstances. Men who want wisdom beg God for this kind of perspective. They constantly ask questions of perspective:

- How will my actions today impact my opportunities next year, my kids in the next decade, and my grandkids in the next generation?

- How will my decisions today affect the opportunities of my company in future negotiations?

- How will my friends' lives be improved by what I'm doing today?

This, in my opinion, is the most fascinating aspect of wise men. I am most inspired by men who have cultivated the ability to see down the hall of history and recognize the far-reaching consequences of today's actions.

Bill Bolthouse is one of these men. I met Bill in the 1980s when I was working as a youth pastor at a church in central California. I had no idea at the time that he was the owner of one the largest carrot producing organizations in the world. Once I found out, I began to take notes on how Mr. Bolthouse ran Bolthouse Farms.

He was committed to honesty in all his negotiations because he believed everything you say today will become part of a future deal. He explained that you have to have a perfect memory to remember your lies, but you can always remember the truth. He ran a 24-hour operation processing carrots and carrot by-products, and he knew he couldn't be there around the clock. So he surrounded himself with people who shared his values knowing they would do what he would do.

Bill hosted a yearly banquet for each shift to thank them for their service and to talk about his personal faith in Christ so everyone knew why honesty, integrity, dedication, and wholehearted focus were his company's values. He didn't require all his employees to believe as he believed, but he understood the clarity that comes to a venture when everyone understands why they do what they do.

Today, "Bolthouse Farms employees over 2,400 people year round and ships over 35,000 tons of carrot products each month."[3] As part of their mission, they quote 1 Corinthians 3:6, "I have planted…watered… but God gave the increase."

Bill has also established a foundation that operates with similar clarity. In 2005 he sold his interest in the Wm. Bolthouse Farms and established the Bolthouse Foundation "to glorify the Lord Jesus Christ by supporting charitable and religious organizations whose ministry, goals, and operating principles are consistent with evangelical Christianity."[4] The foundation has benefited many churches and numerous ministries around the world because Bill had the wisdom to ensure that his influence would live on.

The Short-Sighted Spiral

Unfortunately, many men lack this perspective. They seem unable to discern how their actions this week will change the course of their lives. The clearest area where this is evident today is pornography. First of all, let's face the fact that we are under attack. When I was growing up, men had to go out of their way to expose themselves to any form of pornography. I would have had to go to a store or a club. I would have had to purchase something and carry it with me to gain access to sexually explicit material.

It's different today. There is a multibillion dollar industry[5] aimed at us through our computers. It seeks to gain access, capture our attention, and defile our souls. The assault is on, and you and I are the target. It's amazing how many men are oblivious to the war. Men seem all too willing to fool themselves and are content with a mediocre response to an intense attack. Have you ever tried to excuse your behavior with any of these thoughts?

- A little exposure won't hurt.
- I can handle this.
- I need to know what other men are struggling with.
- I know this is wrong, but I'm sure God will forgive me.
- I'm under too much stress, and this helps me feel better.
- It isn't hurting anyone.
- I haven't noticed any difference in my life.

We all know better. We are all aware that pornography is a poor substitute for intimate relationships with our wives. We all know that we are stimulated by sight and that it's impossible to be focused on God or a healthy relationship while we're viewing explicit material. We all know there is a diminishing effect to pornography. The longer you are exposed to this kind of material the more it takes to create the same response in your mind and body. We all know this intellectually but so many of us seem to lack the understanding that our involvement in these activities will eventually ruin us and everything we hold dear.

In case this is a struggle for you, let me give you my best advice on how to bring this under control so it doesn't become the defining activity of your life.

Admit that it's a problem. A man's sex drive is incredibly annoying and wonderful all at the same time. When we focus the energy toward a healthy, loving relationship, it is extremely valuable. When it's focused on self-gratification and stress relief, it's extremely demanding. There's nothing calm about your sex drive. It is either a great friend or a demanding opponent. When it turns dark, you need to bring it into the light.

Seek out some trusted friends. I can guarantee that you are not alone in this battle. Other men you know are struggling with this and are embarrassed to admit it. If you're willing to admit to your struggle, you can find friends who are also willing to admit to their struggles. Don't be naïve. Not all men are going to want this kind of friendship. You need to pray and seek these friends out. Once you find them, meet regularly. Read books together, study the Bible together, and pray together. Ask each other the hard questions, "How are you doing with pornography? How is your thought life? Did you engage in anything this week that would harm your relationship with God, with your wife, or with your kids?" When the battle is the toughest, soldiers band together.

Invite Jesus into the temptation. Temptation always tries to get us to hide from God. When you invite Jesus into the middle of the temptation, it takes the mystery out of the experience and diffuses the part of the temptation that calls us to hide. I have found that this puts me in a much better position because now Jesus and I are fighting together and I'm no longer trying to do it on my own. It's hard to let thoughts of immorality run wild when you have invited Jesus to be a spectator.

Review often your status as a "set apart" person. The Bible says that as believers, we have been made holy by the saving work of Christ on the cross. This means we have been "set apart" for God, reserved for His praise and service. We now represent Jesus here on earth. We are holy, not because our behavior is perfect but because we are the temple of the Holy Spirit and ambassadors for the gospel. If we view our life in this way, we will make every effort to keep ourselves clean and uncontaminated.

Limit your idle time. All of us need downtime to relieve stress and recharge our hearts and minds for the next battle. Most of us, however, have more of this kind of time than we actually need. The men I know who are most effective plan their downtime. They write on their calendars their work schedule, personal responsibilities, dates with their wives, and activities with their kids. They also write in their leisure activities. They want to make sure they do what brings balance to their lives, but they also want to make sure they aren't sitting around wondering what to do next.

Find a dream big enough to make right choices for. I asked my oldest son when he turned 18, "What do we do well as parents?" His first response was, "You gave me a dream big enough to sacrifice for. You helped me find something to live for that captured my heart." When you have a dream, a passion, a calling that captures your heart, you think twice before you do anything that could ruin what you love. Seeking a big adventure is more than fun; it protects your heart.

Growth in Life Skills

The second area where growth is required is in our *life skills*. The general command to grow is proclaimed in 2 Peter 3:18 while some of the details are addressed in 2 Peter 1:5-9. Peter reminds us all that we are to live a life of addition.

The Attitude of Addition

The phrase "make every effort" has the idea of intense input. "We are to bring 'into' this relationship 'alongside' what God has done every ounce of determination we can muster."[6] If you want to grow, you need to live with the attitude, "I can always do a little better at what I do, I can always learn something more, I can always become more proficient, and I can always progress just a little more."

We don't want to overdue the analysis so that we live with discontent. We do, however, want to live with the anticipation that there is always more to explore, discover, and master. Growth is the attitude that I will press forward until I become the best me that I can be. Growth says, "I want to see how close I can get to my potential."

Then Peter follows up with the challenge, "add to your faith goodness." When I read this casually, I am uninspired. "Be good." I know this is important, but it has never been a driving passion of my life to simply be good. So I decided to look into this further.

The word Peter used here is not the generic word for goodness. Peter is not telling us men to just clean up our act and act right. He uses the word for *moral energy*. "In classical times the word meant the god-given power or ability to perform heroic deeds."[7] These may have been military actions, athletic feats, artistic expressions, or ventures that set people free or inspired others to reach to new heights. Now we're talking. Growth is not simply about being nice, good men who are easier to live with. We grow because we want to do something heroic. We get stronger, smarter, and more skillful because we want to do something that counts and causes others to live bigger lives.

The Art of Addition

Once you've determined that you want to live a heroic, significant life, it's time to develop your skills. Peter gives us the steps when he instructs us to add "knowledge...self-control...and perseverance" (2 Peter 1:5-6). One of the exciting truths of life is that skills are progressive. You are either honing your skills to the point they become second nature or you are watching your skills diminish. They never stay the same. If you have a negative outlook, you will convince yourself it isn't worth trying because you're going to lose what you have anyway. I just can't think of a reason why you would want to think that way. The heroic outlook believes that your skills are going to get better every year because you are going to work on them.

Growing your skills is a work of art in your life. It's not a formula you plug in and robotically repeat. Skills develop because you invest the right stuff and marvel as your abilities get easier and more creative.

It's Your Turn

Before we talk about how to develop your skills, choose a skill you would like to work on this year. Ask yourself, "What do I love to do? What do I want to get better at this year so my influence will increase? What would I like to try to master so that I can enjoy it more?" Write your answer in the space below:

The first step to getting better at this skill is to *acquire knowledge*. If you want to get better, you have to gather information about this area of life. Fortunately, there are a lot of ways to do this. You can read books and magazines. You can research websites, participate in blogs, and join online chat sessions. You can ask mentors and others who have proficiency in the skill you're trying to master. The key is to jump in. It doesn't matter how much you know about the topic today. You can jump in at any level and gain more knowledge.

The first time you hear a concept, it seems obscure and confusing. The second time you hear it, it may still be confusing, but it begins to sound strangely familiar. As you continue to expose yourself to information about this topic, you move from recognition to curiosity to understanding.

As I have mentioned, I enjoy making my house a more comfortable and personal place to live. As a result, I have always bought fixer-uppers. I still remember the first time a friend told me how to install a three-way light switch. This friend might as well have spoken Swahili for all the sense his words made to me. I remember asking, "Why do they call it a three-way switch if it works from only two positions?" I don't remember the answer, but I'm sure he told me something that made sense to him. It was one of those moments that I couldn't even recount to other friends because I understood nothing this man said. I wanted to know, however, because I like working on my house.

So I watched as he wired these switches for me. I asked him to tell me when he was going to install these for someone else so I could watch again. Then I moved into another house, and I found a reason to install a three-way circuit. This time I bought a booklet that showed how to install one. I did my best, blew the circuit, and called my friend to fix my project. Again, I watched him as he corrected my mess.

Then I moved to San Diego and again bought a house that gave me an opportunity to put in one of these funny circuits. This time I went to the Internet and printed out instructions on how these circuits work. For some reason, it clicked this time. I finished the circuit, put in a lightbulb, flipped the switch, and congratulated myself on the light I brought to my family.

You can imagine my reaction when my son called me after he bought his first house and told me he didn't understand why the light in his house that had two switches wasn't working. He had done some remodeling and rewired the circuit wrong. I pulled out my drawings of three-way circuits, talked it through with him over the phone, and figured out the problem. Wow, was I amazed that I now could picture over the phone something I couldn't figure out even in person years before. I laughed when my son said, "Whoa, that was weird, but I'm glad it works."

The second step to developing your skills is *practice*. Peter challenges us to add self-control, which is the mastery you gain over your mind, body, and will through training. The good news about skills is that you get better at them every time you do them. Every skill has a technique that makes it work best, and as you work on your technique, you will improve. No matter what the skill is.

We have a tendency to think of skills as things we do with our body, such as hunting, fishing, woodworking, car repair, athletics, and computer skills. Our skills are not limited to these activities, however. Communication, prayer, Bible study, management, vision-casting, goal-setting, and decision-making are all skills that can be pursued, practiced, and perfected. These are not mysterious talents that some men have while other men got shortchanged. These are skills we can all develop. The problem is that many of these areas intimidate or embarrass us. We don't like to admit that, so we avoid these areas hoping we can get by without improving. This is silly, of course, so it makes sense to dig in, face the possible embarrassment, and work on these skills.

I see this one all the time when I speak at marriage conferences. It's funny to me the statements I hear from men at almost every conference:

- "We aren't going to have to talk to other people are we?"

- "You aren't going to make me share my emotions and stuff with other couples, right?"

- "Tell me I don't have to get up and say anything or I'm just going to go home right now."

- "Can you give me a man card that has the answers to the questions my wife and I have to talk about this weekend? That way I can be ready."

These statements point to the fact that most men have not developed their communication skills. They assume they're just not good at talking because they don't realize it is a learned skill. The first time you work on it, it may be awkward. The second time it will progress to uncomfortable. Somewhere along the way, it will become second nature if you keep practicing.

The third step to developing skills is *finding a reason to make them stick*. Since skills are always progressive, either growing or diminishing, the skills that will last in your life are the ones you develop an internal need for. For this reason, Peter adds the glue to the project of building skills when he calls us to add "godliness...brotherly kindness and love" (2 Peter 1:6-7). Every skill in your life that is motivated by your devotion to God and commitment to other people will last a lifetime and have an amazing impact. When Jesus was asked to describe the greatest commandment, He said that all of what God wants in your life can be accomplished by loving God and loving others as much as you love yourself (Matthew 22:36-40).

When you "trust in the Lord with all your heart...he will make your paths straight" (Proverbs 3:5-6). Inviting Jesus into your skills is like turbocharging your growth; the process is more powerful than you can develop on your own.

It's Your Turn

- What will you do this year to gain more information about the skill you want to get better at?

- What will you do to practice this skill this year?

- Commit the growth of this skill to God in prayer and ask Him to add His power to the process.

Just for Fun

An SR-71 plane was flying across Southern California and entered Los Angeles space. Los Angeles Center reported receiving a request for clearance to FL 600 (60,000 ft.). The incredulous controller, with some disdain in his voice, asked, "How do you plan to get up to 60,000 feet?" The pilot responded, "We don't plan to go up to it, we plan to come down to it." He was cleared.[8]

Chapter 7

Decide to Love

*"Keep it simple. When you get
too complex you forget the obvious."*

—AL MCGUIRE[1]

Angela Schmid shares a story to remind us all of the challenge of loving others: "We rushed our four-year-old son, Ben, to the emergency room with a terrible cough, high fever, and vomiting. The doctor did an exam, then asked Ben what bothered him the most. After thinking it over, Ben said hoarsely, 'I would have to say my little sister.'"[2]

The greatest command that Jesus gave us as men is the command to love: "A new command I give you: Love one another. As I have loved you, so you must love one another" (John 13:34). And Peter picks up the refrain in his first epistle: "Now that you have purified yourselves by obeying the truth so that you have sincere love for your brothers, love one another deeply, from the heart" (1 Peter 1:22).

If you are like me, you have struggled at least a little with this command. At first, it seems a little too soft to be attractive to men. But our Savior called us to a life of love with boldness and without hesitation. So what does it mean to love one another, and how do we do this without minimizing our manhood?

Be a Student of Those You Love

I believe the key to living a life of love is described in Philippians 2:3-4: "Do nothing out of selfish ambition or vain conceit, but in humility consider others better than yourselves. Each of you should look not only to your own interests, but also to the interests of others."

Love means looking out for what is in the best interests of those you care about. You can't look out for the interests of others unless you know what those interests are. Therefore, living a life of love means we must become students of others. We must seek to understand who they are, create opportunities for them to succeed at who they are, and give them grace for who they are.

Everyone you love in your life is different from you. You can't just naturally and instinctively love them. You have to learn what they are about. You cannot just do what works for you and expect that it will be helpful to them.

Gender Matters

> So God created man in his own image,
> in the image of God he created him;
> male and female he created them.
> (Genesis 1:27)

God made men and women different from one another so that He could reflect His image to a world that desperately needs to know who He is. Instead of assigning value to our differences, we have spent way too much time complaining about each other and manipulating our relationships. How many of us can relate to this man's efforts?

After a thorough physical examination, a man said, "Tell me in plain language, Doc, what's really the matter with me?"

"Do you want it straight?"

"Yes."

"Well, there isn't a thing in the world wrong with you except that you're just plain lazy."

"Okay," the patient drawled, "now give me the medical term for it so I can tell my wife."

It's easy for us to get it when it comes to the being male. We're used to the effects of testosterone on our bodies, minds, and attitudes. We may not have attempted to put it into words, but we instinctively understand what makes us feel good about ourselves and what frustrates us.

It's much harder to grasp how the female half of the race operates. We have no idea experientially how estrogen affects life. We don't understand the cycle of menstruation, the emotional vibrancy, or the need to feel safe that dominates their lives. We have no instincts for what makes them feel better about themselves or what frustrates them.

As a result, a strong desire to be on a perpetual learning curve gives you a much greater chance at success with the females in your life.

Let me summarize some of the benefits of each gender by contrasting them with each other.

Males are wired to make things simple.

Our brains were designed so that we compartmentalize our focus. In our book *Men Are Like Waffles, Women Are Like Spaghetti,* Pam and I liken the way we process issues to the surface of a waffle. There are a number of boxes that are separated by walls. We put one issue of life in the first box, a second issue in the second box, and so on. We then focus on one issue at a time. As a result, we are consistently looking for the simplest answers to whatever is in front of us. This doesn't mean we don't like complex things; we just look for the simplest possible solution to whatever we must solve.

I was in a meeting with a group of men talking about what it takes to succeed in ministry. One of the men said, "I've noticed that not many generalists are successful. Men who focus on being specialists and try to become really good at one thing tend to be more successful." This is a typical male way to view a career. We want to simplify our pursuits down to one or two things, and we want to get good at doing those things. We tend to get frustrated when we must juggle too many things, change directions too many times during the day, and deal with too many interruptions. We want to know what the expectations are, and then have the freedom to get them done.

We want romance to be simple. We want to express our interest in the woman we love, and we want our efforts to work. This is why it frustrates us when women "change the rules." We like statements such as, "Any problem can be fixed with flowers or duct tape." If flowers worked last time to make her happy, we want it to work every time. If taking her out to dinner made her feel special this week, we want it to work any time we try it. We are constantly looking for the formula that will win her heart, and we hate it when the prescription doesn't work. We know intellectually it isn't this simple, but we still want it to be this way. It appears to me that most men have just given up on romancing their wives. It seems too hard, too complicated, and their wives appear to be determined to be discontent, so they just quit trying.

We want conversations to be simple. We want to identify the topic of discussion, and we want to stay on subject. We want to settle the issue, and then maybe move on to the next one, or maybe just end the conversation until tomorrow. We like to talk about topics that are simple to us. If we're good at fishing, we like to talk about fishing. If we're good with computers, we like to talk about computers. If we're confident about our knowledge of the Bible, we like to talk about the Bible. Few of us like to talk about relationships because they seem complicated to us. We watch the females in our lives talk about who is seeing whom, who is upset with whom, why that person did that or this person did this, and we wonder why anyone would care.

We are attracted to the hobbies that seem simple to us. If you are adept at working on cars, you tend to like cars and are motivated to spend a lot of time with them. If you find that music comes naturally to you, you will be motivated to spend whatever time is necessary to practice. If you can hit a golf ball straight, you find it easy to spend all day Saturday (or any day) on the golf course. On the other hand, if you golf like I do, you find a whole day on the course to be more like torture than recreation. (I refer to my golf game as spectacular. It's either spectacularly good or spectacularly bad, and it changes with almost every shot.)

If you want to motivate your sons or your friends who are male, you'll want to make things as simple as you can.

Females are wired to make things better.

In Genesis 1:25, "God saw that it [the creation of life] was good." In verse 31, "God saw all that he had made, and it was very good." So what happened between verses 25 and 31 to change things from good to very good? The creation of two human beings, male and female as the apex of God's handiwork. Genesis 2:18-25 then gives us a little more detail about Adam's aloneness and his need for a suitable helper, and about God fashioning a woman from one of Adam's ribs. Adam's response at his first sighting of Eve was to break out in singing.

> "This is now bone of my bones
>   and flesh of my flesh;
> she shall be called 'woman,'
>   for she was taken out of man."

Next time you're tempted to break out in singing when you catch sight of your wife, just remember you're acting like Adam. Eve showed up in a place that was all good, and she made it better by her presence. And thus began the relentless desire in the heart of women to make things better.

They are equipped for this because their brains are wired to integrate their thinking. They process life more like a plate of spaghetti. Each noodle on the plate represents an issue in their lives. Every noodle touches every other noodle, so every issue, every thought, every emotion is connected to every other issue, thought, and emotion. As a result, the way women process information is much different and much more complex than the way men do it. This is why most women can multitask better than most men. They see the connections in life, so they're able to work on more than one issue at a time.

In almost every area of life, a woman's approach is more complicated because everything can be made better. A woman can always look better, even if she is stunningly beautiful. She can always decorate better, even if the house is expertly arranged. She can always organize better, whether her system is efficient or erratic. She can always teach her kids more, help out her friends more, serve more people, or make people happier.

A young man recently asked me, "Why is it that women refuse to be content?" It's because of the nagging, relentless realization that she could have done more because things can always be better. Before you are too hard on the females in your life, remind yourself that your sex drive is a nagging, relentless presence that creates just as much complication and frustration as her drive to make things better.

Relationships are more complicated because women know those relationships can always be better. There is always something that can be worked on, something that can be done better, something that can be understood better. In response, women will either consistently explore their relationships or get overwhelmed by them and withdraw.

I was recently at a social gathering with other couples that Pam and I are close to. The men were sitting in front of the television, watching a football game and talking about football. All we needed in our world at that moment was football. The most complicated the conversation got was when one of the men asked me if I had a fantasy football team. When I told him I didn't, he went on to describe his team and his hopes that his starting quarterback had a good day.

The women were having a much different experience. They were talking about their friends, their kids, their dreams, their frustrations, their makeup, their Christmas plans, the upcoming weddings of their kids and their friends' kids. There were multiple women talking at the same time, and nobody appeared to be lost in the discussion. If you asked any of us men what the women were talking about, we would have just said, "I don't know." If you asked the women what the men were talking about, they would probably roll their eyes and make some comment about the game being on.

It's easy for us men to conclude that the more complicated approach that women take to life is wrong or immature. That's because we don't know what it's like. We find conversations to be strategic, while they find them be recreational. We like to have a single focus on projects, while they like to include all relevant issues and people. We like to simplify things to make them more manageable, while they like to explore things to make them more interesting.

This is why the Bible tells us to "accept one another" (Romans 15:7) rather than "understand one another." It's impossible for a man to fully understand any woman in his life, but that doesn't mean he can't be successful in his relationships. There are many things we don't understand but work with every day. Many men don't understand their cars, but we can all drive. Many men don't understand their computers, but they can work with them. None of us understands love, but most men desire to be in love with a woman and build a life with her. So understanding is not a prerequisite to success, but acceptance is.

To Gender and Beyond

Becoming a student of those you love does not end with their gender. Everyone you know is a fascinating combination of characteristics that results in a unique person. Each of the people you care about is a mixture of inborn traits, learned skills, reactions to life experiences, and the influence of decisions they have made. The people you love determine whether they are valued in your eyes based on your level of interest in these factors that make them who they are. They don't know how to put it into words, but they are aware of when you are interested in them. When you connect with who they really are, their motivation level rises, they feel better about themselves, and they have more energy. They smile more, relax in your presence, and experience a higher level of confidence. They long to be around you because they are better when they are with you.

It would take volumes to fully explain the complex creation of each of your loved ones, so I have no illusions that we can talk about all there is to say. You don't, however, have to be an expert at human development to have great relationships. If you're willing to gain a working knowledge of how people are motivated, you can be a valuable resource in the lives of those who are most important to you.

The Baseline for Motivation

When you go shopping for a new car, you see on the sticker a base price for the car and then options that transform it into the vehicle you see on the lot. In the same way, there is a base starting point for the way each of us is motivated. There are a number of different schemes for understanding this baseline for motivation. (If you are interested in deeper study on the subject, check out the websites in endnote 3 of this chapter at the back of the book.[3]) For our discussion, I will summarize the four basic styles of motivation. As you read these over, try to identify the style that works best for you. Gaining insight into others begins with growth in your understanding of yourself. Once you have a working knowledge of what motivates you, seek to identify the baseline motivation for each of the important people in your life. If your circle of relationships is like most, each person will have a different basic approach to increasing energy and confidence.

Get It Done

The first baseline motivation is all about accomplishments. If this is you, you are happiest when you have freedom to make decisions about where your life is heading, and you have the authority to make them happen. You honestly believe your perspective is right most of the time, and you get confused or irritated when people disagree with you. You love cooperative environments, which means you like to create the environment and you want others to cooperate with it. You are decisive, focused, and forceful in your influence. You see other people as valuable because your ideas are generally larger than you can accomplish on your own. You often say things such as, "I need your help," "I need you to get in gear," "I need you to be more focused," and "I need you to try harder." You aren't trying to be bossy; you just believe that you know what's best, and you want to help everyone get there.

As a result of your visionary ability, you are usually in charge of whatever pursuit you get involved in. You gravitate to the top, and you are most comfortable as a leader. In contrast, you feel awkward when you are required to follow because your understanding of the challenge is usually ahead of whoever is leading.

When you accomplish your goals, you feel great about life and great about yourself. You also feel great about anyone who helped you accomplish what you were reaching for. This is such a strong drive in your personality that you are prone to being bossy when things are moving too slow, irritated when people resist you, disappointed in people when they don't come through for you, and intense when people try to slow you down.

If this is your baseline motivation and you have the privilege of raising children, you need to realize that your son believes he is supposed to be in charge. Your daughter's convinced that she is the best person to lead even when she lacks the life experience to know what's best. If you're going to be effective with these little gifts, you have to raise them with options. You can't just say, "Get dressed," unless you're ready for a confrontation. It's better to say, "There are two outfits on your bed. You need to choose one of them to wear." This gives your little leader the opportunity to choose, which calms down the need to be in charge. Just a note: if your child mixes outfits that don't match, don't worry about it. Peer pressure will eventually take care of this, and you'll have a motivated child to work with.

I recently talked this over with a pastor friend of mine. He has a six-year-old daughter who was born to be in charge. He and his wife have often been frustrated because she screams and runs away when they say to her, "Sweetheart, come here and give me a kiss." They love their daughter and want to shower her with affection, but she keeps resisting them. When I suggested that he needed to give her options, he changed his approach. He went home and said to her, "Would you like to give me a kiss on the right cheek or on the left cheek?" She thought about it for a moment, then walked up to her dad, kissed his right cheek, and gave him a big hug. Then she ran away.

Leaders need options no matter how young they are.

Get It Moving

A second baseline motivation is a desire to create experiences that bring enjoyment to other people. If this is you, you are driven to create memories for people that enhance their lives. You believe life is a journey that's supposed to include laughter, tears, intense victories, fun times, and unforgettable experiences. You are most comfortable up front or in command, but you can work in the assistant role if you truly believe what you are working on will make people happier or more inspired. You live to hear people laugh and find hope. As a result, you are intensely loyal, and you have tireless energy when it comes to making a difference in the lives of those you care about.

Since helping others is what makes you feel alive, you thrive on attention. You love it when people notice you and your contribution to their lives. You have a natural desire to be "a part of the show," so you look for ways to get involved and help run things. You have probably been accused of being shallow because you are looking to keep things moving. When life moves too slow or gets boring, you plan a new activity or round people up for a party, social gathering, or compassionate project. The things that take long conversations, long planning meetings, and long problem-solving sessions are hard for you, so others misinterpret your actions as uncaring or unfeeling.

Since you are intensely loyal, you are confused when other people are not. When others don't finish a project they committed to, you take it personally. When others don't keep promises, you take it personally. When others choose not to attend an event you have planned, you take it personally. Your hurt doesn't last long because there is always a new party or project that people can get involved in to redeem themselves. As a result, you forgive quickly and reintegrate people easily back into your life. You also believe that most issues can be solved with a successful event. A date with your spouse, fun with your kids, or a gathering with friends is like glue to you that fixes problems. Sometimes your efforts to fix everything don't work, but your optimism is relentless, and you will try again and again.

If any of your kids are wired this way, you want to pay special attention to them. They thrive on being noticed and want to know that they bring you hope. That's a big burden for a young person to carry, so these kids are often busier than you think they ought to be, overly concerned with relationships and frustrated because they don't seem to be able to do enough to make enough people happy. They need your guidance and wisdom to set boundaries on their friendships and to learn to prioritize their efforts so their most important relationships get their most productive effort. They resiliently push ahead, so you want to keep moving forward with them and resist the urge to focus on past mistakes, past accomplishments, and past disappointments. Instead, parent them with the hope of better things to come.

Get It Right

A third baseline motivation stems from the belief that there is a right way to do things. If this is you, you are happiest when your life follows the rules. You love principles, procedures, policies, and plans that are followed. Once you set your mind on a way of doing things, you will commit tenaciously to it until someone can prove there is a better way. In fact, you see little reason to change unless there is a compelling mandate to do so. You see great value in routines, rituals, and repetition. After all, if it was right the last time, why would you want to do it any different this time?

Life is a lot more organized because of you. Things are easier to understand and easier to find because you have brought order and consistency to life. You've helped us harness the power of technology and systems. You've helped us manage our time better, discipline our lives better, and maintain order in our homes. Without your influence, we would all be too spontaneous, too unstructured, and too self-absorbed to reach our potential.

All who love to get it right have a primary task they must accomplish.

In your pursuit to figure out how life really works, you are evidence collectors. You are consistently seeking to grasp the reality of things. You have the ability to collect positive evidence that enhances your faith and leads to thoughts such as, *Wow, God sure has been good to us. We have our health, we seem to have the wisdom we need for the next decision, and we are getting along well.*

Too often, however, you collect negative evidence as you spiral into frustration. We live in a broken world, so it's easy for you to see the shortcomings and to run disaster scenarios in your mind. It's all too easy for your thoughts to spiral down. *Life has been hard and will probably get harder this year. We have moved out of crisis and appear to be heading for an all-out disaster.* Once you start spiraling down, it's possible to keep spiraling unless you establish a bottom that turns your thinking around toward hope.

The good news is that we have been created with the ability to choose an activity that can serve as a bottom to the spiral. *First*, it must be a task. Those who want to get it right are task-oriented by nature, so they are moved by doing things, not just hanging around. It could be an exercise routine you engage in, a CD or playlist that you listen to, a trusted friend you call, or a routine you put into action.

Second, you'll want this task to be the same each time. Once you have found an activity that turns your thinking from negative to positive, you'll want to repeat it every time you need it. Repetition is vital because you are wired for routines and positive rituals. Using a habit as the bottom also keeps you from having to think about what you'll do when you become too introspective, which will help you avoid the overanalyzing that comes all too easy to you.

Third, assign to this task the ability to stop the spiral and turn your thinking toward God's blessing and the possibilities of life. God has given us the ability to choose, so we can choose to turn our thinking, our attitudes, and our focus.

Let me give you two examples of how this works. Steve is a get-it-right friend who is committed to his family and his career. He came to me one day after church and said, "Bill, you need to pray for me."

"What's going on?" I asked.

"I lost my job."

"I'm sorry to hear that, Steve. You look upset. Did you get fired or laid off?"

"I got laid off."

"Did they not give you a severance package? Is that why you're so upset?"

"Oh, yeah, they gave me a severance, but it's only for nine months."

I wanted to say to him, "Dude, you scored. You've got nine months to figure things out. You can reinvent your career in that time. Man, don't blow this." But I knew that would trivialize his struggle. I knew him well enough to realize he was on the spiral down. He had already run the disaster scenario. He had envisioned himself never finding another job, losing his home, and living with his loved ones under a bridge begging for food. I made it my goal to help him find a bottom to this spiral.

"Steve, get your PDA out," I said.

He immediately pulled his electronic calendar out of his back pocket.

"On what date will your struggle go critical? When will your family's needs get insurmountable if you have trouble finding work?"

He told me the date, which was about six months away. I then told him to find that date on his calendar, which he did, and to make an appointment for that date.

"Write on that appointment, 'Start to Worry,'" I said.

He looked at me a little puzzled, and then wrote his assignment on the appointment.

"If you get to that date and you still haven't found work, worry as much as you want," I said. "Feel free to worry intensely, lose sleep, and whine if you want. Until then, you don't need to worry because you have your worry date picked out."

A month later, he approached me again and said, "Bill, you'll never guess what happened."

"You found a job, didn't you?"

"How did you know?"

I didn't really know, but I figured that if he took all the energy he was using to worry and turned it in a positive direction, he would seek work with energy, interview with confidence, and present himself as someone who would add value to anyone's organization. It was just a guess, but it seemed like a logical guess.

Another couple approached me about their son. "Derrick has an anger problem," they said. "Do you think you could meet with him and see if you can help?"

At the meeting with Derrick, I realized he did not have an anger problem. He was a get-it-right kind of person, and things were not right in his home. His parents were under a lot stress, and they were not getting along well. Derrick was absorbing the stress, trying to figure out how to make it right. Each time he thought about his family he would spiral down until it overwhelmed him. In frustration, he would erupt in anger.

I explained to him how some people get caught in downward spirals that make them frustrated and mad. By the nodding of his head, I could tell he recognized that he was one of these people. I asked Derrick, "Can you tell when the spiral starts in your mind?"

Fortunately he could, so we designed a "stop, drop, and roll" program for him. I suggested that as soon as he became aware of the spiral, he should shout out loud, "Stop," roll on the ground three times, and then end up on his knees and pray, "Jesus, what do You want me to do next?"

This simple routine worked to put Derrick's emotional energy back under his control. It helped him to laugh about his life and to feel a little more power in the midst of their family stress. It worked so well for him that he put a "stop, drop, and roll" poster on the refrigerator, his bathroom mirror, and his closet door. His family grew to expect that at any time, Derrick might unexpectedly stop, drop, and roll.

Get It Together

A fourth baseline motivation grows out of an inward drive to be part of a team. These people want to do life together. If this is you, you enjoy life most when you are a part of something. You function best when you make decisions together, work on projects together, seek solutions together, and spend time together. For you, life is about "we" much more than "me." Because the team is so important to you, you are easy to approach, and your perceived needs are relatively low. You are much more comfortable helping others than being helped. You reserve your energy for the together times, so you tend to be easy-going and low maintenance. You are motivated by statements such as, "It's awesome to have you around," "We all function better when you are involved," "Our life is better when you are with us," and "It's great to have you on the team."

Your satisfaction comes from helping other people succeed. When you are convinced you've had a hand in boosting another's influence, prosperity, or personal growth, you think to yourself, *This is what I was born to do*. When people ask you what your vision is for your life, your first response is, "I'm still working on that. What's yours?" You are motivated by exploring what fires up others and brainstorming ways to make it happen together.

Others like to be around you because you are encouraging, engaging, and relaxed. You listen well, negotiate well, mediate well, and value everyone's input. You tend to have a lot of wisdom because you've been part of many teams throughout your life and you've learned from each of them, but you tend to hold back your opinion until you've been asked. Your opinions are often disregarded because you lack natural fire in your soul and your ideas come across as too tame. You may be the first one to be aware of a fire, but people don't respond because you calmly report, "The house is on fire," rather than shout, "Fire! Fire! Get out of the house *now*!"

A good example from history of a get-it-together man is Barnabas. The first time we meet him, he has just sold a field and given all the money to the church to help those in need (Acts 4:36-37). The next time we encounter him, he's introducing Paul to the apostles (Acts 9:27). Paul was notorious for arresting believers and turning them over to be executed. Word had spread that he had been converted in dramatic fashion, but his reputation made it hard to believe. Barnabas saw the integrity of Paul's faith and used his influence to open a door of acceptance for the greatest church planter in history. In Antioch, Paul and Barnabas formed a team and "for a whole year Barnabas and Saul met with the church and taught great numbers of people" (Acts 11:26).

When it was time for the church at Antioch to send out a team to plant churches, the Holy Spirit said, "Set apart for me Barnabas and Saul for the work to which I have called them" (Acts 13:2). As part of the team, they chose a young man named John Mark. This young man started out well, but then he quit halfway through the trip and returned home (Acts 13:13). In Acts 15, Paul, who is a get-it-done man, approached Barnabas with the idea of taking a second missionary journey to expand the influence of the gospel. As they discussed who their teammates should be, Barnabas suggested they take John Mark.

Paul basically said, "He's a loser, and he will never again be on my team." Barnabas's opinion was different. He saw this young man's potential and believed he could recover from his past mistakes. The two had such a sharp disagreement over John Mark that they parted ways. Paul partnered with Silas and hit the road while Barnabas returned home to Cyprus with his protégé (Acts 15:36-41).

From this point forward in Acts, we don't hear anymore about Barnabas. We know that Paul had a successful ministry, but we are left to wonder about Barnabas's influence. We do, however, know that he continued to be effective because John Mark is the author of the book of Mark. Barnabas helped him recover, rebuild, and refocus to the point that his words have influenced every generation since with the truth about the life of Jesus. Helping John Mark succeed was more important to Barnabas than his own fame because he considered Mark an important part of the team.

Those with a get-it-together approach don't like to be defined by what they do. They live to be part of the team and to belong to a significant group of people. They thrive on acceptance for who they are and on the respect they receive for their contribution to the team. When you define them by personal achievements, their motivation drops off.

When our youngest son was in elementary school, his grades had fallen below what we knew he was capable of. We put together a plan in conjunction with his teachers to bring his grades back up. At the first progress report, his grades had improved, so we said to him, "Caleb, we're so proud of you. You're doing great and working the plan with skill. Way to go."

At the next progress report, his grades had dropped again, and we were confused. We had a good plan, we were giving positive feedback, and we had the right people on board. As we talked with him, it occurred to me that the problem was with his lack of motivation, so we changed our approach. We called Caleb into our living room and said to him, "We want you to know that we love you and we always want you to do your best, but mostly we want you to know that our life is better because you are around."

Now, if you are a get-it-done man, you're probably thinking, *Our life is better because you are around? What kind of weak, namby-pamby, sissy talk is that? We need to get that boy on task and work the laziness out of him.*

All I can tell you is that since we committed to affirm him as a vital member of our team, we've had no problem with motivation. His grades were high throughout high school, he served in student government, he was president of the Fellowship of Christian Athletes' huddle at his school, and he was the team captain for both football and track. Since we told him we wanted to get there together, he got it together.

It's Your Turn

In the space below, write down the names of the most significant people in your life. Then mark how you would characterize each of them: Get It Done (motivated by accomplishment and control of decisions), Get It Moving (motivated by attention and creating memories), Get It Right (motivated by the process and routines), or Get It Together (motivated by being on the team). Then write down a couple of ideas for each of them that you can do this month to raise their energy level.

Name 1:

Baseline Motivation:
- ☐ Get It Done
- ☐ Get It Moving
- ☐ Get It Right
- ☐ Get It Together

What I can do this month to motivate this person that I love:

Name 2:

Baseline Motivation:

- ☐ Get It Done
- ☐ Get It Moving
- ☐ Get It Right
- ☐ Get It Together

What I can do this month to motivate this person that I love:

Name 3:

Baseline Motivation:

- ☐ Get It Done
- ☐ Get It Moving
- ☐ Get It Right
- ☐ Get It Together

What I can do this month to motivate this person that I love:

Name 4:

Baseline Motivation:

- ☐ Get It Done
- ☐ Get It Moving

☐ Get It Right

☐ Get It Together

What I can do this month to motivate this person that I love:

Just for Fun

Golfer Tommy Bolt was famed for his oddball antics and mercurial temper. Endeavoring to enliven a golf clinic one day, Bolt asked his teenage son to "show the nice folks what I taught you."

The boy excitedly grabbed a nine-iron—and threw it into the sky.[4]

Chapter 8

Decide to Be a Friend of God

"Impossible is just a big word thrown around by small
men who find it easier to live in the world they've been
given than to explore the power they have to change it."

—MUHAMMAD ALI[1]

There is a special privilege reserved for those who are willing. It started with Abraham, who was asked by God to do the unthinkable—sacrifice his one and only son. This was the son promised to Abraham when both he and Sarah were too old to have kids. This was the son on whom all the promises hinged. This was the son on whom Abraham's family's future rested. And God asked Abraham to offer him up.

In a remarkable act of faith, he took the trip with Isaac, made the altar, arranged the wood, and sharpened the knife. In the most intense conversation of his life, he explained to his son the call God had placed on him to offer up his son in an awful act of obedience. The moment the steel of the blade was about to contact the flesh of Isaac's neck, God intervened and called off the sacrifice. Abraham's journey to the brink of sorrow resulted in his being called "God's friend" (2 Chronicles 20:7; James 2:21-23).

It is understandable that God would call Abraham His friend; he is the one man who understood what it meant to willingly sacrifice his one and only son. God the Father knew He would have this same experience later in history, so there was a special bond between Abraham and his God. The opportunity to be a friend of our Savior does not end with Abraham, however.

Job described his relationship with God in terms of friendship. In his attempt to explain the tragic state of his life, Job said these words to the other friends who were challenging him: "Oh, for the days when I was in my prime, when God's intimate friendship blessed my house" (Job 29:4). Then, in an almost unbelievable offer, Jesus said to His disciples, "I no longer call you servants…Instead, I have called you friends" (John 15:15).

It seems too casual, too generous, too far-fetched that the God who is infinitely beyond us would want to build such camaraderie with us. And yet, this is what He has said.

Friendship Takes Time

So, what does it take to build a friendship with God? The process is described in John 15. It begins with spending time together. It's impossible to be a friend with someone you never spend time with. It starts small and then grows as the relationship develops. "I am the vine, you are the branches" (v. 5). Without argument, Jesus is the strong one in the relationship, just as the vine is stronger than the branches. The branches start off small. As they "spend time" with the vine, they grow and ultimately flourish. In the same way, a friendship with God builds step-by-step until it becomes a flourishing companionship.

Spending time with Jesus begins with the spiritual disciplines that help us "remain" in Him (vv. 6-7), but it is not limited to formal activities. Spending time with Jesus is also casual and more organic. This is where you invite Jesus into your hobbies, your recreation, your entertainment, and your common struggles. You experience life together.

What do you like to do? What do you do to have fun? You may love to hunt or fish. You may enjoy working on cars or working in your yard. You may love technology or tools or tinkering around. When was the last time you invited Jesus to join you in one of these activities?

One hobby I enjoy is working on my vehicles. As I get lost in the project, the stress of life seems to disappear. I especially like the satisfaction of the finished project. I like to walk around it, look closely at it, and marvel at the beauty that appears. Working on a car is so different from my professional life that it acts as an escape for me. My car has no emotional issues and makes no demands when I work on it. There are no deadlines except the ones I decide to impose.

If I want to be a friend of God, it makes sense that I invite Him to join me when I work on my car. I have, therefore, decided to ask Jesus to be involved in my car projects. Before I begin, I pray, "Jesus, what do we want to work on today? We could work on the wiring, the body, or the brakes. Do You have a preference?" In the midst of the project, I often pray, "Jesus, You are much smarter than I am. Do You remember where I put the tool that I need right now?"

It's common on these projects to run into stripped bolts, broken parts, and human mistakes. I used to get frustrated with these and blurt out some shout of irritation. After I invited Jesus to join me, I decided I probably didn't want to do that. These setbacks are still frustrating, even with the awareness that Jesus is present. It would be silly to say, "Wow, Jesus, I just cracked my knuckles on the side of the engine block, and now they're bleeding. Thank You that I could share this experience with You." Instead, I've learned the secret of intense prayer at moments like this. "Oh, Jesus, that one hurt. You probably saw that one coming. No, don't laugh at me; it hurts. I know, the crucifixion was much worse, but this hurts."

I also enjoy working out. I grew up running and playing, and I participated in high school athletics. As a result, working out feels normal to me, and I like my life better when I'm in decent shape. I also have the challenge of having athletic boys, so there's the male ego to factor in ("I can keep up with these young bucks"). It would be easy for me to compartmentalize this activity, but I want to have a friendship with my Savior, so I invite Him to work out with me. I have learned from my 23-year-old, who is a strength and conditioning coach, that my workouts should be varied to create "muscle confusion" or my body will get used to the effort I'm putting in and minimize the results. So I've created a list of possible workouts I can do each day, and before I begin I ask God, "So what workout do You want to do today?" I also have praise music and an audio Bible that I listen to when I exercise to transform my mind as I train my body.

It's Your Decision

What do you like to do to relax or have fun?

Brainstorm ways to invite Jesus to be a part of this activity in your life.

The Common Struggles

Friendship with Jesus gets supercharged when you decide that He ought to be involved in the common struggles of your life. I learned this principle from my good friend Jim Conway. Jim has been a pastor, seminary professor, conference speaker, and consultant. He currently oversees a ministry called Midlife Dimensions, an interactive website (midlife.com) that helps men and women with their midlife transitions. Jim is one of the boldest men I have ever met, so it's common for him to ask me questions that break down defenses and get to the core of life. He is also one of the most transparent men I have ever met.

We were talking one day about the struggle all of us men have with lust. We admitted to the fact that God made women beautiful. We also conceded that God gave men an aggressive sex drive that must be managed. He then said to me, "One of the things that's helped me is a simple, direct prayer. Whenever I see a woman and the engine begins to rev, I say to Jesus, 'Please meet the need in my life that I think this woman could meet.'"

It was stunning to me when I first heard it. I had already memorized the main verses dealing with lust because I wanted victory:

> "I made a covenant with my eyes
>> not to look lustfully at a girl."
>>> (Job 31:1)

> Do not lust in your heart after her beauty
>> or let her captivate you with her eyes,
> for the prostitute reduces you to a loaf of bread,
>> and the adulteress preys upon your life.
>>> (Proverbs 6:25-26)

> "You have heard that it was said, 'Do not commit adultery.'
> But I tell you that anyone who looks at a woman lustfully

has already committed adultery with her in his heart" (Matthew 5:27-28).

> It is God's will that you should be sanctified: that you should avoid sexual immorality; that each of you should learn to control his own body in a way that is holy and honorable, not in passionate lust like the heathen, who do not know God (1 Thessalonians 4:3-5).

Even with these verses committed to memory, the struggle did not change. It didn't get worse; it didn't get better. I was just stuck in a disciplined struggle to keep lust under control so it didn't become the defining action of my life.

Then I began to pray the way Jim had suggested, and things started to improve. It ignited something within me that had been lying dormant. I looked at the passage in 1 Thessalonians 4 again to see if I could discover the secret of why this was working. Verses 4 and 5 jumped out at me: "that each of you should learn to control his own body in a way that is holy and honorable, not in passionate lust like the heathen, who do not know God." For the first time, I saw the difference. Those who acted in passion did not know God. By implication, those who learn to control their bodies do know God. The way to get stronger against lust was to invite God into the struggle.

I admit that what I really wanted to do was overcome the challenge by my own power and ingenuity. I wanted to discover the plan that would lead to victory, implement the plan skillfully, and then report to Jesus so He would be impressed. But I had nothing impressive to report. All of my efforts to live "holy and honorable" produced no progress.

It was different when I let Jesus be my friend in the struggle. Asking God to meet the need in me took the mystery out of the temptation. It didn't seem as attractive when I transparently admitted to my Savior that I was human. Realizing that most temptation is the belief that a legitimate need can be met in an illegitimate way made the need more attractive than the temptation.

Talking to Jesus about the need to be loved, accepted, respected, complimented, and desired was powerful. It made me feel valuable and alive. I no longer had to deny the passion in my soul and the desire to be treasured by another human being. Instead, I could fully admit to these drives and brainstorm with my Creator ways to meet these needs without disappointment. It isn't like a magic button that takes the struggle away, but inviting Jesus to join me in the midst of the challenge has led to progress that I believe will continue as long as I want it to.

I have since discovered that this doesn't work just with lust. My other most common struggles are: (1) I quickly get anxious when I think there isn't enough money to cover my responsibilities; (2) I procrastinate making phone calls when I believe they are going to be unpleasant; and (3) I am prone to get angry when it feels like my life is being controlled by someone else.

I am confident these are areas that will require attention for the rest of my life, but I have made much progress since I asked Jesus to get in the middle of the growth. When I tried my best to get better, progress was at a standstill. When I asked my Savior to join me in my common struggles, I began to mature.

It's Your Decision

What are your most common struggles?

Right now, invite Jesus to join you in the midst of these struggles. Then remember to reinvite Him anytime you're aware that the struggle has gone active.

Friendship Thrives on Loyalty

In John 15:13, Jesus told His followers, "Greater love has no one than this, that he lay down his life for his friends." With your true friends, you do what it takes to defend their honor, help them succeed, and protect them from harm. In essence you lay down your life for your friends. Jesus did this for us because He values the relationship. He humbly laid down His glory to experience life on earth just like us. He humbly laid aside His powers to go through the same process of living that we do. Finally, He humbly laid down His life on the cross so that He might pay the price for our sins, for which we lack sufficient resources to pay (2 Corinthians 5:21; Philippians 2:5-11; Hebrews 4:15-16).

It is now time for us to respond. We need to look for ways to express our loyalty to Him by defending His honor, joining Him in the great commission, and choosing Him and His ways over anything that would seek to take His place. We live in a world that regularly criticizes the name of Jesus. If we are His friends, we will speak up and defend His honor regardless of the inconvenience or criticism it produces. Defending His honor begins at a personal level as you stand for Him in your circle of influence.

I remember the first time somebody told me that Jesus is a crutch that weak people use to get through life. My first thought was, *This guy is totally ignorant of what a real relationship with the Savior is all about.* I said to him, "So, I guess you don't know."

"I don't know what?" he responded with a quizzical look.

"I guess you don't have any idea what it's like to have a real relationship with Jesus. Either that or you must think a crutch is like a turbocharger."

"A turbocharger? What are you talking about?"

"Knowing Jesus is the most exciting thing that's ever happened to me. He's the author of life and the greatest source of personal power on earth. He knows everything about you, and He's committed to making you the best you can be. He'll move you faster toward your potential than you dreamed possible. When you meet Him, He fills you with motivation, strips you of limitations, leads you to new opportunities, and saturates you with wisdom. You can't possibly meet Jesus and limp through life because He loves to run."

He didn't really like my answer, but I wasn't content to let his opinion hang in the air. Jesus is the best friend I've ever had, and I was determined to defend His honor.

There also are times for public proclamation. Because we live in a world that is hostile to the things of God, we must band together sometimes to stand for what is true. Most recently, we battled in California to maintain God's definition of marriage. Proposition 8 was a tough fight with passionate supporters on both sides. Opponents of Prop 8 tried to characterize the issue as one of hatred and discrimination. In reality, they were trying to redefine the truth and supplant God's standards. It was God who made us male and female. It was God who said "a man will leave his father and mother and be united to his wife, and they will become one flesh" (Genesis 2:24). Some people try to reduce the truth of Scripture to just another opinion rather than bow to Jesus as the Creator and King of life. I am thankful that in this case the church rose up, banded together, and reestablished the sanctity of marriage.

Pam and I attended the celebration at city hall after Prop 8 passed. The crowd of supporters was well-behaved and enthusiastic. Pastors and other community leaders made speeches in respectful tones, expressing their gratitude to those who sided with God's plan. A group of people who opposed the measure gathered nearby with megaphones. We were called "Christian terrorists," compared to Nazis, and told that we were hate mongers. They claimed to be tolerant, but their criticisms proved they were anything but. We stood our ground and finished our celebration because we knew they were fighting against our friend, Jesus, and we stand with our friends.

What areas of life is Jesus asking you to stand with Him, to be His friend?

It's Your Turn

Take time right now to thank Jesus for laying down His life for you.

How can you defend the honor of Jesus this week?

Listen to Advice When It Is True

Jesus' words, "You are my friends if you do what I command," must have sounded strange to His disciples (John 15:14). This was their rabbi, their leader, their teacher, and the hope of their future. They were not used to thinking of the authority in their lives as a friend. Jesus, however, understood that a part of friendship is giving and receiving advice. Your friends observe you in many different settings. They see the best in you, the worst in you, and the mediocre in you. There are times when your friends possess the perspective that you need. Healthy friends, therefore, accept advice from their friends when they are right.

Jesus has a decided advantage over all of us because He is always right, so any advice He gives are the right words for the right time. That is why He says, "Do what I command." It's not that He wants an unhealthy level of control in our lives; He is just right about what's best for us. He wants a real friendship with us where we exercise our will and utilize our gifts. He wants us to bring the best we have to the relationship, just as He brings His best to our lives. It is awesome to have a friend like Jesus because we seldom can see far enough ahead to know what we should do. At these times, Jesus steps in, makes His opinion known, and pushes hard on us to obey.

I will never forget the first time I was aware that Jesus was doing this in my life. I was a 19-year-old student at California Polytechnic State University, San Luis Obispo, and I was active as a student leader in Campus Crusade for Christ. I attended a student leadership conference at the headquarters of Campus Crusade, and I went with the anticipation that I would receive training in being a better leader and would interact with other leaders who would sharpen my skills. I never dreamed I would meet the woman who would become my life partner.

The first time I saw her, I was sitting with my best friend, Scott, waiting for a meeting to start when three young ladies approached us and asked, "Do you know Jim Farrel?" They asked because Scott and I were wearing hats that were similar to one my brother wore at a conference earlier in the summer where two of the three women had met him. When I told them he was my brother, they began to scream. Then Scott said to one of the women, "Aren't you Phyllis and didn't I go to third grade with you?" At that, they screamed even more, and Pam (my future wife) silently excused herself and returned to her seat.

It was the next day at the pool that I first really noticed Pam. She was a diver at her college, and I admired her skill on the diving board.

She was also really cute. I thought to myself, *I'd like to get to know her as a friend.*

We interacted casually during this conference, but nothing more than a friendship developed. At another conference later that same year, we had a couple of serious conversations about how God was working in our lives and what our future goals were. These conversations raised my interest in her, but I still wasn't thinking there was anything but a friendship developing.

At the Christmas conference in December, I asked her to join my brother and me, along with a number of other friends, on a group date. I was pleased she said yes, but I had no idea that it would hit me the way it did. The next day I attended seminars, but I couldn't concentrate. I was frustrated and exhilarated all at the same time. I knew I had to do something or this conference was going to be a waste of my time.

I asked Pam if I could talk to her that night after the conference activities. I said to her, "I'm having a hard time concentrating, and I think I really like you. Are you okay if we spend time getting to know each other better?"

I didn't know what to expect, but I had to take the risk. Many decisions are this way. You know you must decide. You have enough information to move forward but not enough information to know exactly how it will turn out. Based on the evidence, you move forward hoping it's the right move, and you wait to see what will happen.

Fortunately, Pam responded well. She seemed pleased that I wanted to spend more time with her and that I was so upfront with her. For the rest of the conference we spent all of our free time together, and a romantic relationship began. We lived two hours apart from each other, so our dating life consisted of me driving to her hometown, where I stayed with a friend while I spent time with Pam. She would then drive to San Luis Obispo and stay with a friend there while we spent time together.

We had lots of questions about life, but we both knew for sure that serving Jesus was the most important thing in our lives. We loved each other, but we didn't want anything to interrupt our ability to serve God for the rest of our lives. As a result, we were willing to stay together if that enhanced our ministries, and we were willing to let each other go if that was necessary. The following summer, Pam was going to attend a two-month Bible college in Colorado, and I was going home to work. We decided to use these two months to commit our relationship to prayer. To ensure that we focused honestly, we decided not to communicate with each other during those two months. I drove to Bakersfield to say goodbye to Pam, and then headed to my parents' home, which was a two-and-a-half-hour drive. As I started home, I began an agonizing argument with God.

"God, I really love this woman, but I can't get married yet. I'm 20 years old, I drive a green Vega with a blue back door, and I own only two pairs of pants. Did I also tell You that I have no real job, and one of the pants has a hole in the knee? I want to do Your will, but I'm not ready to get married."

As long as I prayed this way, I had a knot in my stomach. I could feel the tension in every muscle of my body, and my stomach hurt. The discomfort caused me to give cooperation a try. "Okay, God, I'll marry the woman." As soon as I prayed that, God caused His peace to wash over me. The tension was gone, and the cramp in my gut disappeared.

It was unsettling for me, however, so I took up my cause again, telling God how young I was and how unprepared I was to take on the responsibility of a wife. I guess I was expecting a different result this time, but the pain in my gut returned and the tension took over once again. My hesitation was based on my desire to be in full-time ministry. I had played out the scenario in my head about what happens when people get married young. I expected that I would marry Pam, she would get pregnant, I would have to commit to a job that I didn't really like to provide for my family, and I would never finish my education. It seemed to me that this would make it impossible to ever get into full-time ministry.

God would not let up, however. We went back and forth for two hours. I was trying to convince Him that this was not the right time, and He kept overwhelming me with stress when I wouldn't cooperate and overwhelming me with peace when I would.

I finally said to Him, "I can't argue with You anymore. I'm afraid this decision means that I will never be in full-time ministry, but it's too hard to resist You. I'm committing today to marry Pam and see how it turns out."

This is the way some of your most important decisions in life work. You assess the risks, you weigh out your options, and you commit to what you believe is the best course of action. There is always a risk. There is always the possibility that you may fall flat on your face and have to talk about failure as part of the story line of your life. It is equally possible that you will soar because of this decision and talk about it as one of the best moves you ever made.

Things moved quickly when Pam got back from Bible school. We talked in mid-August, got engaged on August 26, and were married on December 14, 1979, at the age of 20. Once I committed to the decision, the emotional trauma disappeared. I embraced the challenge and set out on the journey to figure out how to be the best husband I could be. I read books, asked other men who seemed to have successful marriages, and listened to radio programs that talked about marriage and family.

Looking back, it's easy to see that God intended to rebuild Pam and me together because of the ministry He had planned for us. We learned together how to serve in our church. We learned together how to communicate. We learned together how to forgive. We learned together how to make marriage practical. Much to my amazement, we supported each other as we finished two bachelor's degrees and a master's degree.

It's Your Turn

What advice is Jesus trying to get you to pay attention to?

Tell Jesus about something you enjoyed doing this week.

Friends Share What They Know

Jesus invited His followers into a deeper level of friendship when He said, "Everything that I learned from my Father I have made known to you" (John 15:15). Jesus would never be content with His superiority. He knew, and His disciples knew, that He was smarter, wiser, stronger, and more talented than they were. He could have shown off and humbled them every time they got together. He could have overwhelmed them with His reasoning, overshadowed them with His talent, and overstated their lack of maturity. Instead, He told them He would share with them what He had learned. He wanted His friends to benefit from what He had learned through His relationship with God the Father.

In the same way, Jesus wants to share with us what He knows. Consider just a few of the things God has said He wants to pass on to you:

- He wants to share "great and unsearchable things" (Jeremiah 33:3).

   "Call to me and I will answer you and tell you great and unsearchable things you do not know."

- He wants to teach us how to be effective servants (John 13:13-17).

   "You call me 'Teacher' and 'Lord,' and rightly so, for that is what I am. Now that I, your Lord and Teacher, have washed your feet, you also should wash one another's feet. I have set you an example that you should do as I have done for you. I tell you the truth, no servant is greater than his master, nor is a messenger greater than the one who sent him. Now that you know these things, you will be blessed if you do them."

- He teaches us what is true and right (1 John 2:27).

   As for you, the anointing you received from him remains in you, and you do not need anyone to teach you. But as his anointing teaches you about all things and as that anointing is real, not counterfeit—just as it has taught you, remain in him.

- He wants us to know His Father (Matthew 11:27).

   "All things have been committed to me by my Father. No one knows the Son except the Father, and no one knows the Father except the Son and those to whom the Son chooses to reveal him."

- He wants us to be aware of our purpose and our attitudes about living out that purpose (Philippians 3:14-15).

  I press on toward the goal to win the prize for which God has called me heavenward in Christ Jesus. All of us who are mature should take such a view of things. And if on some point you think differently, that too God will make clear to you. Only let us live up to what we have already attained.

- He wants us to know how God thinks (1 Corinthians 2:9-13).

  However, as it is written:
     "No eye has seen,
        no ear has heard,
     no mind has conceived
        what God has prepared for those who love him"—
  but God has revealed it to us by his Spirit.

  The Spirit searches all things, even the deep things of God. For who among men knows the thoughts of a man except the man's spirit within him? In the same way no one knows the thoughts of God except the Spirit of God. We have not received the spirit of the world but the Spirit who is from God, that we may understand what God has freely given us. This is what we speak, not in words taught us by human wisdom but in words taught by the Spirit, expressing spiritual truths in spiritual words.

It is not a one-way friendship, however. Jesus wants us to share with Him what we know also. I know this sounds ridiculous because Jesus already knows everything that we know. He doesn't need to learn anything. He doesn't need to be instructed in anything. He will never need to ask any of us a question. But friends share what they know because they enjoy the interaction.

This is why throughout the Bible we are encouraged to interact with God. "The prayer of the upright pleases him" (Proverbs 15:8). "Your Father, who sees what is done in secret, will reward you" (Matthew 6:6). "Jesus told his disciples a parable to show them that they should always pray and not give up" (Luke 18:1). "Pray in the Spirit on all occasions with all kinds of prayers and requests" (Ephesians 6:18). "Do not be anxious about anything, but in everything, by prayer and petition, with thanksgiving, present your requests to God" (Philippians 4:6-7). "Devote yourselves to prayer, being watchful and thankful" (Colossians 4:2). "Pray continually" (1 Thessalonians 5:17). "For the eyes of the Lord are on the righteous and his ears are attentive to their prayer" (1 Peter 3:12).

Jesus is so interested in having an interactive relationship with us that He is even willing to compete with our wives. When Paul was writing to the church in Corinth, he told married couples to periodically use the time they would otherwise engage in sexual activity and use that time for prayer. "Do not deprive each other except by mutual consent and for a time, so that you may devote yourselves to prayer. Then come together again so that Satan will not tempt you because of your lack of self-control" (1 Corinthians 7:5). He doesn't intend for this period of abstinence to be permanent, so he calls us back to intimate relations. But wow, what a way to get our attention! I'm pretty sure that none of us is in danger of having his sex drive go dormant. In the same way, Jesus wants us to keep our desire to spend time with Him vibrant and aggressive.

Jesus even knows that at times we have no idea what to share with Him. We realize He knows everything and we know almost nothing in comparison. He knows that life is manageable for Him and often overwhelming for us. He sees all of the future, so He is able to put the pain of life in perspective. We are limited in our perspective, so we often get knocked off stride by the pain. At these times, God still wants to hear from us, even when we don't have anything to say. "In the same way, the Spirit helps us in our weakness. We do not know what we ought to pray for, but the Spirit himself intercedes for us with groans that words cannot express" (Romans 8:26).

I recently went through an experience in which I needed Jesus to share His perspective with me. It involved my purpose, and my attitude about how I was going to live out this purpose, in the next season of life. I knew in my early twenties that my purpose was to serve God in ministry. I don't think full-time ministry is any more important than other pursuits, but it was the pursuit that captivated my heart. Since that early calling, I spent eight years working with teenagers in a church in central California, fifteen years preaching and leading a church in San Diego County, and three years building a small group ministry. Along the way, a ministry of writing books and speaking developed. It was a part-time pursuit for me but a full-time pursuit for my wife.

Then came the call in 2007 to travel full-time speaking at conferences and churches. On the surface, this sounds like a great calling. Travel the country, speak about things I'm passionate about, spend lots of time with my wife. The challenge is that this is a ministry my wife has run full-time for years, and I was entering her world. I don't know about you, but it has never been a dream of mine to work for my wife and have her teach me how to be successful. I know that we are partners and that it takes my gifts and her gifts to make our ministry go, but the truth wasn't all that clear when I first made the move. I felt out of my comfort zone in many areas as I gained new skills and learned new ways to live life and serve God.

I told Jesus, "I know I told You I would do anything and go anywhere for You. I actually meant it when I prayed that prayer. I just didn't think it would be this. I always thought that I would be a part of a local church and that Pam and I would speak part-time. Obviously, that's not the plan anymore. I need a verse that I can hang on to during this transition. I am fascinated by this challenge, but there's much about doing this full-time that's not clear to me. Can You give me something that will help?" Shortly after this prayer, I came across Psalm 32:8:

> I will instruct you and teach you in the way you should go;
> I will counsel you and watch over you.

I was instantly encouraged. God was reminding me that He was committed to instructing me, teaching me the way I should go, counseling me, and watching over me. It was a stark reminder that my purpose was intact and it was being led by the one who authored that purpose in me. I said to Jesus, "Thanks. That is awesome. I asked You to give me something obvious and that is exactly what You did. You know my friend often says to You, 'I don't do hint,' and I needed You to deal with me that way. Thanks again." Then I kept reading:

> Do not be like the horse or the mule,
>   which have no understanding
> but must be controlled by bit and bridle
>   or they will not come to you.
>   (Psalm 32:9)

I couldn't believe it. Jesus had just called me stubborn. He compared me to a horse or a mule who doesn't want to follow his owner. I couldn't help myself at this point. I pictured Jesus putting a bit in my mouth and running the reins up over my head. I could either follow willingly or He could yank on the reins to get me to comply. I was going to follow either way. The only question was, "Would I follow the easy way or the hard way?"

I would love to tell you that I've been a willing follower ever since, but the reality is that He has had to pull on the reins more than once and I "shared" with Him my opinion of His aggressive leadership. I'm just glad that Jesus has given me freedom to have an open relationship with Him. Meeting Him was the greatest moment of my life, and I would do anything for Him. It just makes the journey a lot more enjoyable knowing that my Savior is my friend who faithfully leads me even when I am stubborn.

It's Your Turn

What would you like to share with Jesus that you've been holding out on?

Friends Open Doors of Opportunity for Each Other

"You did not choose me, but I chose you and appointed you to go and bear fruit—fruit that will last. Then the Father will give you whatever you ask in my name" (John 15:16). Jesus proclaimed His commitment to help us harness the opportunities of life. When we pursue Him as a friend, we will bear fruit and receive from God the Father "whatever we ask in his name." This is not a license to engage in self-absorbed pursuits while we leverage God to do what we want Him to do. Rather, it's the natural result of solid friendships.

When I see an opportunity that's good for one of my friends, I tell him. When I find a pursuit that's big enough for others to experience also, I tell my friends about it. When I know of a training conference that is high quality, I invite my friends to join me. I want my friends to know about anything that's helping me be a better man. If I can figure this out with my friends, surely Jesus has it figured out with us.

How about the other side of this friendship? How do we provide opportunities for Jesus? It sounds like a strange question doesn't it? How could the Creator of the world need anyone to open any doors of opportunity for Him?

Strategically, it isn't necessary because Jesus has no needs, but relationally He has made it possible. He has set up a partnership for evangelism. We know that salvation is a gift of God, but we have been called to be the messengers: "How, then, can they call on the one they have not believed in? And how can they believe in the one of whom they have not heard? And how can they hear without someone preaching to them? And how can they preach unless they are sent?" (Romans 10:14-15).

As we share our story of faith, support the ministry of our church, engage in outreach activities, and pray for our friends who do not know Jesus, we help the cause of evangelism. We cannot change people's hearts, but we can provide opportunities for the name of Jesus to be known because He is our friend.

It's Your Turn

What verse has God given you for the year ahead? (One way to discover a verse is to go to www.biblegateway.com and plug in a few key words on the topic you are looking for. A list of choices will appear, and you'll be able to select one. Write that verse out in the space below.)

Just for Fun

A young and nervous preacher was asked to hold a graveside burial service at a pauper's cemetery for an indigent man with no family or friends. Not knowing where the cemetery was, he made several wrong turns and got lost. When he eventually arrived an hour late, the hearse was nowhere in sight, the backhoe was next to the open hole, and two workmen were sitting under a tree eating lunch.

The diligent young man went to the open grave and found the vault lid already in place. Feeling guilty because of his tardiness, he preached an impassioned message, sending the deceased to the great beyond in style.

As the preacher returned to his car, one workman said to the other, "I've been putting in septic tanks for twenty years and I ain't never seen anything like that."[2]

Chapter 9

Decide to Be a Man of Principle

"People never improve unless they look to some standard
or example higher and better than themselves."

—Tyron Edwards

The world is desperately looking for men of principle. Men who speak truthfully and do the right thing because it is the right thing. One of the men who has inspired me from a distance is Mike Krzyzewski, the highly successful head basketball coach of Duke University and a man of humility. I am impressed with his ability to train young men to play at the peak of their performance while maintaining a cool, focused demeanor most of the time. Coach K once said, "The truth is that many people set rules to keep from making decisions."[1]

Principles require decisions. You can follow a rule without thinking. You can robotically do what you are told without engaging any imagination or exercise of your will. You can be numb and follow a rule. You must be vitally engaged in life to apply principles to real situations.

This is the focus of a life of grace. The Old Testament contained an intricate set of laws that defined the requirements of a holy God. It was communicated to men to lead them as a tutor to the truth about grace (Galatians 3:23-25). The law taught us that none of us are perfect no matter how hard we try. That realization was intended to build a hunger in each of us for a Savior who would forgive us and share with us His power for living.

This is what was accomplished in the gospel. Jesus paid what you owed for your imperfection. He rose from the dead so He can have an active relationship with you today. He placed the Holy Spirit within you so His power for life, decision-making, and relationships could be available to you around the clock. In the process you've been adopted into the family and given the charge, "Live as children of light" (Ephesians 5:8).

Now we are free in Christ. Not free to do whatever we want, but free to choose the best of all possible actions because there is no guilt and no condemnation in our choices. There are only consequences. Every choice we make affects our lives in some way. Some choices impact life positively while some have a negative influence. Some choices alter life long-term while some create only short-term ripples. If you are a man of principle, you will make decisions that will have the most positive impact for the longest period of time.

Developing Your Skills

Before we discuss the primary principles that guide life, we need to discuss the skills that are required to be a man of principle.

Delayed Gratification

We've all been created with senses that profoundly affect who we are and how we live. It is because of these senses that we love to eat. It's amazing to me how good some food can taste. Eating homemade spaghetti sauce with sausage is almost a religious experience for me. It is nearly impossible for me to have ice cream in the house and not eat it. Barbecued chicken with pesto sauce and lemon juice makes my mouth water just writing about it.

It is because of these senses that we love entertainment. A good movie, television show, or event can captivate our attention and keep us spellbound for hours. Conversely, we can react with great emotion when we are confronted with an entertainment option we don't like. I love being married, but I don't love chick flicks. I love watching football games and movies with action and suspense. After seeing one movie recently with my son, he said to me, "Wow, that was great. It makes me want to drive really fast on the way home." (This was in contrast to what one of my other sons said a year ago after we had watched a highly acclaimed movie together: "Well, that's two hours of my life I'll never get back.") We react this way because entertainment connects with our senses and moves us emotionally.

It is because of these senses that we love sex, physical affection, strenuous activities, listening to music, hiking in the forest, working in the yard or in the garage, and closing the deal in business. We love to feel the intense reactions testosterone creates in us to the things we love most.

Our senses, however, are not a friendly ally. They can be recruited by either side of our nature. The dark side of our nature is recruiting our senses to gratify the flesh as fast and as often as humanly possible. The new nature in us is recruiting our senses to enhance our lives for the long haul. The new nature is aware that life is eternal, while the old nature is concerned only about today. The new nature takes a wide view into the unknown, while the old nature narrows its focus only to what it sees.

This became more than a theory to me during my wife's first pregnancy. I was sitting on the couch one day thinking about becoming a dad, and I suddenly had the urge to start explaining to my unborn child all the great experiences that were waiting for him or her. Everything from great meals to jet skiing to laughter with friends to projects that reflect your personality. I wanted to describe sunsets and fast cars and the thrill of competition. As I was thinking about this, it occurred to me that my unborn could never understand these things no matter how hard I tried to explain them. He did not have the capacity to grasp the concepts or descriptions. All this child could do was trust me as I unfolded these experiences over time.

That was when I realized heaven is like that to me. Jesus can try to explain it, but I don't have the capacity yet to understand. All I can do is trust Him to unfold the experiences in due time. My job is to learn to wait until the time is right.

If you are like me, "Wait" is your least favorite command in the Bible. I like "Go." I like "Focus." I like "Charge." "Wait" is a different story, and "wait patiently" is even harder to swallow. But I can never be a man of principle if I need to be gratified today. If I don't learn how to put off my rewards, I will never be able to objectively evaluate my decisions. Unless my long-term success is more important to me than short-term indulgence, I will sacrifice my principles for what feels best to me today.

It's Your Turn

To help stretch out your ability to wait, practice saying these phrases to yourself:

- I would rather please God than men.
- I am willing to wait for my reward in heaven.
- Long-term success is better than short-term success.
- What I will experience in eternity is worth waiting for.
- I can wait.

To energize your ability to wait, try one or more of these exercises:

- Fast one day a week for a month.
- Give the money you would normally spend on entertainment in one month to a missionary or charity.
- Physically run away from a temptation when it presents itself. I mean *run*. If you are on your computer and are tempted to go to a website you know you shouldn't, get out of your seat and run outside. If you are walking and are tempted to look again at a beautiful woman, run to the other side of the street. If you are tempted to go back for another plate of food at the buffet, pay your bill and run to your car.
- Save for six months to buy something you want rather than put it on your credit card.

Tenacity

Men of principle have cultivated the dedication to finish what they start. They believe life is important and must, therefore, be pursued with focus and determination. It doesn't matter how long it takes to finish. It doesn't matter how much effort it eventually takes to finish. Men of principle are satisfied when they finish quickly, but they are just as satisfied if it takes multiple tries to get it done. They are tenacious.

Without tenacity, you open yourself up to the possibility of compromise. Rather than doing the right thing, you'll do the easier thing. Rather than follow your principles, you'll opt for a diversion that meets a more selfish agenda. The good news is that you can cultivate tenacity so that finishing what you start becomes a habit.

One of the most inspirational examples in my development was

Archie Griffin, running back for the Ohio State Buckeyes. He played college football while I was playing high school football, and I took an intense interest in following his career.

When he was 12 years old, he was nicknamed "Tank" because he was, in his own words, "short and fat." He wasn't content to accept that as his lot, however, so he tenaciously did something about it. He began lifting weights, which consisted of two cases of beer bottles filled with dirt attached to a mop handle. He turned his family's bathroom into a steam room and encased his body in plastic cleaning bags to lose weight. He did sit-ups in the family station wagon with three sweaters on during the summer. He brought this same tenacious attitude to high school football and started as a sophomore.

His dad, James Sr., recalls, "I never knew Archie had streamlined himself into a back until I saw him play his first game that year. I remember he ran off tackle for a 50-yard touchdown, but they called it back because of an offside penalty. So on the next play he ran 55 yards, but they called it back again. So then, darned if he didn't run 60 yards, and this time the refs must have got tired, because they gave him the touchdown. I remember saying to one of my older boys, 'Man, we got something here.'"[2] His coach recounts that Archie played the last three games of his senior year with a broken bone in his foot, and "they still couldn't catch him."

His beginning at Ohio State wasn't quite so glorious. The first game he played in was against Iowa. The Buckeyes were in command of the game 21-0 late in the fourth quarter when they decided to give their fifth-string freshman running back an opportunity. Griffin quickly fumbled the pitch for a five-yard loss. After the game, Griffin was listed on the freshman roster and was relegated to the practice squad.

During the next game against North Carolina, Ohio State coach Woody Hayes was frustrated with his ineffective and underachieving offense. To send his starting players a message, he decided to put the fifth stringer into the game. Griffin was so surprised, he ran onto the field without his helmet. An assistant coach had to call him back to give him this vital piece of gear. By the time he came out of the game in the fourth quarter to a standing ovation, Griffin had gained 239 yards (an OSU single-game rushing record) and led the Buckeyes to victory.

He never gave up his starting position after that and is the only man in NCAA history to win the Heisman Trophy twice.

Archie Griffin is an obvious football legend, but his tenacity does not allow him to live in the shadow of accomplishments already attained. His coach called him the greatest player he had ever seen, but Archie gives all the credit to God, his teammates, and his coaches. A fellow player, Pete Johnson, said about Griffin, "He thinks he's a nobody. Archie is probably the only person who doesn't know he's Archie Griffin."[3] He didn't settle for being overweight. He didn't settle for being small (5'8", 185 lbs). He tenaciously stayed at the task until it was finished.

Compassion Wrapped with Thick Skin

If you are going to be a man of principle, you'll need to have compassion, because our purpose in this life is to help others become their best. Men of principle care about people. But people are needy and inconsistent. They will thank you one day and blame you the next. They will want what you have to give them, but then they will criticize you, disrespect you, and malign you.

The master at having compassion wrapped in thick skin is our Savior, Jesus. Jesus ministered to the world even though "he came to…his own, but his own did not receive him" (John 1:11). He knew that men would never come to Him on their own, so "while we were still sinners, Christ died for us" (Romans 5:8). Jesus demonstrated His deep concern for mankind when He wept because of the pain death had brought into the world (John 11:35). He was not naively compassionate, however. Jesus knew He could not trust the things that people said because they can turn in a hurry. "He knew what was in man," so "when they hurled their insults at him, he did not retaliate" (John 2:25; 1 Peter 2:23).

If you want to live by principles then, you must be prepared to be criticized and opposed by the people you are seeking to help. This does not mean that everyone you try to help will be difficult. In fact, most people will be appreciative and complimentary. Some, however, will make you out to be the devil himself, even though you have done the most good for them. Men of principle don't like this, but it doesn't change their convictions, their commitments, or their resolve.

Anyone who has a dream of making a difference will be criticized, even when that dream is to improve the lives of others.

- Winston Churchill's father concluded that his son was "unfit for a career in law or politics."

- George Washington's mother was enraged by his commitment to command the American army because she believed it was his duty to stay home and take care of her.[4]

- Steve Jobs and Steve Wozniak, founders of Apple Computer, were told by Hewlitt-Packard, "Hey, we don't need you. You haven't got through college yet."

- Fred Smith was told by the U.S. Postal Service, UPS, and his business professor at Yale that Federal Express would fail.

- Decca Recording Company in 1962 said about the Beatles, "We don't like their sound, and guitar music is on the way out."

- In 1861, Johann Philipp Reis was told in Germany that there was no market for a telephone, so he shouldn't waste his time developing one.

- Lord Kelvin, president of the Royal Society said, "Heavier-than-air flying machines are impossible."

Criticism is inevitable but it is no reason to give up on compassion. The world needs what you have to offer.

It's Your Turn

On the chart on the next page make a list of projects or commitments you have started but have not finished. For each item, project a deadline of when you'd like to be done. Stay flexible here because these are your deadlines. The goal is to make yourself more tenacious.

Project/Commitment	Projected Deadline

Choose how you want to respond next time someone you are trying to help criticizes you:

- I am obviously making a difference in this person's life.

- I don't like this, but I refuse to let this knock me off track.

- Jesus, thank You that I get to experience a small dose of what You experienced.

- I will push a little harder to help someone this week.

- I will help someone else who appreciates my efforts more than this person.

- _____

Picking Your Principles

Once you've determined that you will live by principles, you have to decide what those principles will be. Your principles are the ideas and convictions that you believe are true regardless of the circumstances of life. You will always live out your principles because they are the deep-seated beliefs you hold in your heart that express themselves in your behavior. This is a bigger challenge than it appears on the surface because we live in a world that runs on a different system. The world system is self-absorbed, short-sighted, and characterized by:

- the goal to get rich (1 Timothy 6:9-10)

- deception (Colossians 2:8; 1 Thessalonians 5:4-7)

- jealousy, which leads to quarrels (1 Corinthians 3:3)

- trivial pursuits to meet everyday needs (Luke 12:30)

- pride (James 4:6)
- control over others (Matthew 20:25)

Each of these characteristics is subject to change. Since the primary goal is self-gratification, men who adhere to this system will manipulate, deceive, and change tactics to suit their needs. They hold to schemes that can change and will say whatever is necessary to gain an advantage. They are hard to figure out because their so-called convictions are moving targets.

You live in this world, so you face a daily barrage of opinions, schemes, arguments, negotiations, and training that encourage you to join the show. When you live by principle, you run counter culture, and those in the culture will make sure you know that they oppose you. Jesus said, "Broad is the road that leads to destruction, and many enter through it. But…narrow the road that leads to life, and only a few find it" (Matthew 7:13-15). For most of my life I pictured these two roads as parallel paths that veered off in different directions. My thinking was transformed when I pictured the narrow road going in the opposite direction in the middle of the wide road. If you are on the narrow road, it's obvious to everyone that you are going the other direction. At every encounter they criticize you and make fun of you as they lobby you to turn around and join them.

Tell the Truth

When our boys were young, my wife and I began to talk about how to develop character in their lives. We decided to focus on one character trait each year so that it would be easy to remember. We wanted to keep things simple enough that they could succeed and focused enough that we could hold them to it. As we talked about where to start, we both agreed that the most strategic principle of life is honesty. If our boys would tell us the truth, we would be able to trust them. We could count on them and talk over issues with confidence. If they weren't honest, we would need to constantly evaluate our interactions with them to determine if we were being manipulated or if they were being cooperative.

We told them, "Brock, Zach, and Caleb, honesty is important to us. We want to know that what you are telling us is true, so you'll get in twice as much trouble for lying to us as you will for anything else you do wrong."

They didn't like it at first, but they learned that we were serious about this principle. Zachery gave us the biggest run for our money because he liked to have things his way. We were working on our house one day and had filled an ice chest with drinks and candy. By the afternoon, Zach had reached his quota of chocolate, so we told him, "Zachery, no more candy for you today. Do you understand?"

He nodded yes, but I could tell by the look in his eyes that he was already scheming. Sure enough, about an hour later I watched as he bent over the ice chest and looked around to see if anyone was watching. I find times like this amusing. I could see every movement he was making, and yet he acted as though he were hidden. As soon as he put more candy in his mouth, I shouted, "Zachery, put that candy down." I met him at the ice chest and marched him to a room where we could be alone.

"Zach, did you eat chocolate when you weren't supposed to?" I asked him.

"No, I didn't," he said as chocolate ran down his chin and dripped on the floor.

"Zach, I can see the mess on your chin. So I'm going to ask you again, did you eat more candy?"

"No," he said with even more conviction in his voice.

"I'm going to have to discipline you now because you are lying to me." I gave him a spanking and then turned him around to ask again, "Did you eat more chocolate?"

"I did not take candy!" he shouted. "Leave me alone."

It took me about an hour of talking and disciplining to get through to him. I finally had to isolate him from everyone else (he absolutely loves being around people) before his heart would change and he would admit that he had disobeyed and then lied about it. I knew it was a battle I had to win or he would learn that he could lie and get away with it.

I have noticed that grown-ups are a lot like kids when it comes to telling the truth. We like the truth when it's comfortable and helps us out. We don't like the truth so much when it makes us look bad or requires us to have to clean up a situation. Men of principle tell the truth whether it's comfortable or not.

Stay Under Control

Self-control is the ability to focus the powerful forces of your life in a healthy direction. You have passions, desires, and dreams that are relentless. They must be steered by something or they will wreak havoc in your life. A man of principle will want these strengths to be active, but he will be committed to having them under control rather than letting them run loose. Consider the prominence of self-control in the following Bible verses:

- Older men are challenged to be self-controlled (Titus 2:2).
- Older women are challenged to train younger women to be self-controlled (Titus 2:4-5).
- Younger men are challenged to be self-controlled (Titus 2:6).
- The Holy Spirit works to develop self-control in the followers of Christ (Galatians 5:22-23).
- All who walk in the light rather than the darkness are challenged to be self-controlled (1 Thessalonians 5:6-8).
- Everyone who has a relationship with Christ is challenged to be self-controlled (1 Peter 1:13; 4:7).

Wherever the writers of the New Testament talk about the principles we are to live by, self-control is part of the list. It really is an incredible grasp of the obvious. It's impossible to live by principles if you don't have self-control because every time you apply a principle to life, you direct your attitudes and behavior. You can direct these actions only if you have self-control. Otherwise, you are operating by instinct simply reacting to your impulses. Self-control is the conviction that I ought to say yes to some things because they enhance my life, and I ought to say no to other things because they diminish my life.

Do What Needs to Be Done

Wayne Gretzky is considered by most to be the greatest hockey player ever to lace up skates. He is the only player to reach 200 points

in a season, and he did it four times in five years. He held or shared
61 National Hockey League records when he retired in 1999 and was
inducted into the NHL Hall of Fame that same year. In talking about
what it takes to live by principles, he said, "Procrastination is one of
the most common and deadliest of diseases, and its toll on success and
happiness is heavy."[5]

Gretzky succeeded because he took initiative. He did what needed
to be done as soon as he was aware of what needed to be done. I am
not sure why procrastination is so common among men because most
men I know are doers. They think aggressively, they laugh loud, they
work hard, and they dream big. And yet, putting things off and ignor-
ing things that need to be done is epidemic.

When I was working as a youth pastor, Pam and I visited the home
of one our families. As we were talking, the mom said to her 17-year-
old son, "Tim, the trash needs to be taken out."

There was no movement out of Tim. He didn't respond, he didn't
get out of his seat, and he looked mildly offended.

"Tim, did you hear me?" she said. "The trash needs to be taken out."

"I heard you, Mom," Tim said in that sarcastic tone only teenagers
can do justice to. "Do you really want me to stop talking to our youth
pastor right now?"

(Isn't it amazing how teens know exactly how to use their parents'
words against them?)

"Okay, so when will you take the trash out?"

"I'll do it as soon as Bill and Pam leave," Tim said.

At the end of our visit, we ended up standing in the kitchen talking a little longer than we'd planned. As we were talking, Tim's mom
picked up the kitchen trash can and placed it at Tim's feet. We finally
said our goodbyes and walked to the door. Instead of picking up the
trash can, Tim just stepped over the container and walked to the car
with us. I'm still not sure he ever took the trash out.

Then I became a dad, and I noticed this same disease lurking in my
three boys. We challenged them regularly to notice what needed to be
done and to do it. It was amazing how much effort they put into not
having initiative. I would walk by the bedroom door and ask, "Hey,
look at this. What do you think needs to be done with this room?"

Whichever one I asked would say, "The room needs to be cleaned." But there was no action. They didn't say, "I'll get right on that, sorry you had to point it out." They didn't say, "I was hoping you wouldn't notice. I was so busy cleaning the garage that I had to put off cleaning my room. I was going to get after it this afternoon, but you looked before I could start."

I wish procrastination was limited to kids, but I have seen the same infection spread among the men I know. They have plenty of initiative for the areas they are comfortable with, but they act as if they are being punished when confronted with areas of discomfort. Check out some of these remarkable statements I've heard from capable men:

"I hate doing dishes. I've been willing to let maggots appear rather than clean up the sink."

"I love my wife, but I wish she didn't talk so much. She wears me out with her words, so I just keep myself busy in the shop."

"I don't understand why my boss makes such a big deal about us getting to work on time. I always get my work done. What does he care when I do it?"

"I knew I should've gone to the doctor sooner. I didn't want him to do those really creepy tests, so I just gutted it out."

"My kids drive me crazy. All they want me to do is play with them. Don't they know I have important things to do?"

All of these situations could easily be remedied. Dishes take only a few minutes to clean. Wives who get consistent attention tend to be more reasonable about how much they talk. Employees who show up on time get better treatment than those who show up late. Health issues are much easier to keep under control when you catch them early and stay on top of them. Kids who get their dad's attention are much easier to discipline and reason with. All of these actions take only a little bit of time, but they more than make up for the time later on.

Men of principle do what needs to be done without having to be asked.

Keep Your Promises

One of the great things about being men is that we can choose to make as many or as few promises as we want. We can limit the number of commitments we make, or we can make lots of promises and load up our lives with commitments. It's up to each of us.

Whether you make lots of promises or just a few, men of principle keep their promises. They do what they said they would do. They stick to their commitments, period. They love it when things turn out well, but they don't give up when things turn out difficult. John Wooden, legendary coach of the UCLA Bruins, used to tell his players, "Things turn out best for the people who make the best of the way things turn out." Men of principle keep their promises because they are promises, not just because they improve our lives.

I believe we are moving away from being a society of principle. Even the most conservative statistics point out that 40 percent of marriages end up in divorce.[6] These are people who publicly said, "I will be with you until one of us dies." It appears they didn't really mean it. Kids who now have to learn to live with two homes, two families, and four parents have become commonplace.

Our government leaders regularly make promises to get elected that they have no intention of keeping. Contracts no longer hold the same weight as a handshake used to. Those of us who choose to keep the promises we make will, therefore, stand out. We will be encouraged to compromise and told we are naïve for sticking to our commitments. We will be lobbied with the idea that our happiness is the most important thing. We may even be tagged with criticisms such as old-fashioned, rigid, out of touch, or judgmental. The question we must all wrestle with is, "Do I keep promises because I am a man of principle, or do I keep promises only when they're easy?"

John Wooden is one of my all-time heroes. I watched with wonder as his teams won 10 NCAA titles in 12 years. It was actually my dream to play basketball for the Bruins while I was growing up. I would spend hours on the court pretending to be Lew Alcindor (he later changed his name to Kareem Abdul-Jabbar), Sydney Wickes, Marques Johnson, or Gail Goodrich. Other than the fact that I was too short and too slow to actually get a scholarship, I had everything I needed.

I watched with great attention as UCLA won 98 straight home games at Pauley Pavilion. But as I matured, I gained even greater respect for Coach Wooden because of his integrity. UCLA was actually his second choice. He wanted to coach for the University of Minnesota because he and his wife wanted to remain in the Midwest. Stormy weather in Minnesota prevented him from receiving the scheduled offer over the phone. John thought they had lost interest, so he accepted UCLA's offer. Shortly after, Minnesota got through and offered Wooden a position. He declined because he had already given his word to the Bruins.[7]

That's the kind of man I want to be.

Respect Everyone

Principled men accept that every man is unique in his talents, but all men are equal in value. As a result, men of principle go into every conversation, every negotiation, every disagreement, and every meeting with an attitude of respect. I consider respect to be the conclusion that everyone I interact with is as important as I am. They, therefore, deserve to be treated with humility, patience, courtesy, and prayer.

The Bible declares, "Bless those who persecute you...Live in harmony with one another. Do not be proud, but be willing to associate with people of low position...Do not repay anyone evil for evil" (Romans 12:14-17). Barry Sanders, the great running back for the Detroit Lions, puts it this way, "Maybe a good rule in life is never become too important to do your own laundry."[8]

Woody Hayes won 13 Big Ten titles and 3 national championships in 28 years at Ohio State University. He was tough on his players and pushed them hard. Most people don't know that every Thursday after practice he would take a group of players to Children's Hospital to visit kids in the burn unit or who were having other health problems. He arranged to have a backdoor entrance so the press wouldn't know about this activity.[9] He wanted his players to respect all people so they wouldn't get too enamored with themselves.

Jesus had important work to do on earth. He had 12 disciples to train. He had truths to teach. He had a plan of salvation to fulfill or all generations would be lost without any hope. The disciples wanted to protect their rabbi's important agenda, so when people brought their children for Jesus to pray for them, the disciples "rebuked those who brought them." Rather than commend His disciples, Jesus told them to stop holding the kids back and to let them come to Him (Matthew 19:13-15).

Jesus knew He couldn't build His ministry on children, so He spent most of His time with His disciples. He also knew that children, and their parents, were just as important as the disciples were, so He took time to pray for them. He knew that if you cannot respect the "least of these," you will never become one of the greatest.

It's Your Turn

Choose one of the principles below to work on this week. In the space below, write down three steps you can take to help establish this principle in your decisions:

☐ Tell the truth

☐ Stay under control

☐ Do what needs to be done

☐ Keep your promises

☐ Respect everyone

Step 1:

Step 2:

Step 3:

Just for Fun

Michael Leamons reminds us that sometimes it's best to say no: "Although desperate for work, I passed on a job that I'd found on an employment website. It was for a wastewater plant operator. Among the job requirements: 'Must be able to swim.'"[10]

Chapter 10

Decide to Be a Role Model

*"People seldom improve when they have no
other model but themselves to copy."*

—OLIVER GOLDSMITH[1]

Nichelle Nichols played Lieutenant Uhura in the hit TV series *Star
Trek*. After the first season she complained to one of her fans that
she was being underused and minimized. She shared that she was planning to leave the show and would make her announcement the following week.

Her fan responded to the news, "You cannot. Don't you know who
you are? Don't you know what you have? Don't you know you're a
part of history? You're opening a door that can never be closed. You're
changing the face of television forever. Nichelle, you cannot leave."

The fan was none other than Dr. Martin Luther King Jr.[2]

Don't You Know Who You Are?

Dr. King's words show the power of role models who are willing
to get involved and share their hearts. Lieutenant Uhura became a fix-
ture on the popular TV show and opened up doors of opportunity for
many others. The course of Nichelle Nichols' life changed because of
the influence of one of her role models.

In the same way, there are people around you who are watching
how you live and listening to what you say. They want to be like you
because they like what they see in you. They admire the way you live,
and they believe they can be better if they imitate your attitudes, mannerisms, and decision-making.

I hope this is good news to you because this is normal. Jesus told

His disciples, "I have set you an example that you should do as I have done for you" (John 13:15). Paul told his readers, "Follow my example, as I follow the example of Christ" (1 Corinthians 11:1). Peter told his readers, "Christ suffered for you, leaving you an example, that you should follow in his steps" (1 Peter 2:21). He challenged those who wanted to be leaders to be "examples to the flock" (1 Peter 5:3).

This is just how life works. Those who admire you observe you and evaluate their lives against your example. I was making an announcement in church one day. "Men, I want to remind you that this Saturday we're going to have a men's breakfast. We'll have eggs, sausage, and pancakes. We'll have a guest speaker, and this is a great opportunity to bring friends and make some new friends. So I will see you this Saturday at seven a.m."

My oldest son was sitting on the front row taking it all in when he spontaneously erupted, "Dad, how are you going to make it? You're never up that early."

I don't know what was funnier, his statement or the shocked look on my wife's face. It was a reminder to me that although he had his facts wrong, he was watching. He thought he knew my schedule and he sincerely wondered how I was going to be in bed and at the men's breakfast at the same time.

When my youngest son was old enough to listen in church, he started sitting in the front with my wife. I noticed that he imitated everything I did. If I pointed, he pointed. If I lifted my hands, he would lift his hands. I learned from him that I had a habit of touching my ear when I was searching for a thought during a sermon. He was so intent on doing exactly what I was doing that the church started watching him instead of me. Pam had to move him to the back so I could do my job, but it was another reminder to me that my kids consider me a role model.

The Benefits

Being a role model is good for us. It keeps us honest. Our instincts for giving other people advice tends to be clear. We seem to know what's best for our friends. The instincts we have for giving ourselves advice are not quite as good. It's amazing to me how often we do things we would never recommend to others.

I am confident J. Paul Getty would not recommend to anyone else his response to the death of his son Timmy at age 12 of a brain tumor. Getty was on a business trip in Europe and refused to return to attend the funeral. He wrote in his journal that day, "Funeral. Sad day. Amoco up 2 and ⅞, Gulf down 1 and ¾." Amazingly, when his dog developed cancer, Getty flew home immediately and spent three days weeping in his pet's room after he passed away.[3]

Nobody who takes time to think about it would recommend you ignore your sick son but then mourn over your dog. But this kind of thing happens all too often. We don't mean to be shortsighted and we didn't set out to be selfish. We just didn't listen to the advice we would have given to others.

When you decide that you want to be a role model, you evaluate your decisions differently. If you think no one is watching or that your decisions are only about you, you will tend toward selfishness. You will be concerned only about how you are affected. When you care that others are watching, you ask questions such as, "How will my life today affect my kids? How will my friends' lives turn out if they do exactly what I'm doing? Would I encourage the people I care about to do what I'm about to do?"

My kids' lives are more important to me than my life. If someone has to struggle, I would rather it be me. If someone has to sacrifice, I would rather it be me. I want my kids to be more successful in their pursuits, more mature in their growth, less stressed in their challenges, and have better relationships than I do. It has helped me in my journey to keep them in mind with every decision I make and before every statement I make. Trying to help them be stronger young men has made me a stronger man.

The other big benefit of choosing to be a role model is that you become more effective. As we all know, people respond more positively to what you do than to what you say. Look at your circle of friends. You have developed similar mannerisms without setting out to do so. My friends and I love fist bumping, but we never talked about doing it. It just happened. When my kids were playing high school football, their head coach had a habit of making a certain face when he was skeptical about something. His lips would tighten while his head turned slightly to the right and his left eyebrow would rise. It was weird to notice this last year that all three of my sons have the same mannerism. This coach passed on his reaction without ever saying, "Hey guys, I want you to learn how to do this."

In the world of words, we have varying degrees of influence. You may be a man who is smooth with words. You may be a man of few words. You may be a man who talks a lot but struggles to communicate what you're thinking. In the world of actions, however, we are all equal. Our kids notice what we do. Our grandkids notice what we do. Our friends notice what we do, and those who consider us as mentors notice what we do. And those who notice begin to do what we do. Therefore, regardless of how well you handle words, your example will highly influence others.

Of course, this either works for you or against you. Robert Downey Jr.'s first brush with the law occurred in August 1996. He was stopped for speeding but ended up being arrested for drunk driving and possession of heroin. His first encounter with drugs, however, took place when his father offered him a marijuana joint at the age of eight.[4]

Do Your Best

Fortunately, you are not required to be perfect to be a role model. You know as well as I do that that's not possible. You have learned from others as they simply lived out their lives in front of you. To be a role model, you simply need to be you. To be a good role model, you will want to be the best you that you can be.

This is a consistent theme in the biblical passages that talk about being an example. For instance, before the apostle Paul challenged the Corinthians to follow him (1 Corinthians 11:1), he laid the groundwork by saying, "whether you eat or drink or whatever you do, do it all for the glory of God" (1 Corinthians 10:31). When he encouraged the Philippians to "join with others in following my example" (Philippians 3:17), he also said, "I press on toward the goal to win the prize" (3:14). This is his way of saying, "I am doing my best, so join me in doing your best also." He knew he wasn't perfect, so he admitted, "Not that I have already obtained all this, or have already been made perfect" (3:12). He had a lot to learn and a lot of growing to do, but people were still following.

When Paul was explaining to his protégé, Timothy, the realities of ministry, he said his life was an example of the "unlimited patience" of Christ. He considered himself to be the worst man who had ever lived because he had tried to snuff out the gospel by killing those who were following Christ (1 Timothy 1:15-17; Acts 9:1-22). His life was an example of God's ability to transform His enemies into useful men. Paul, therefore, challenged Timothy to do his best in public speaking, in life decisions, in loving others, in believing God, and in living a morally excellent life. He was convinced that as Timothy did his best, God would change others' lives through his example (1 Timothy 4:12).

You are probably intensely aware of your shortcomings. At the same time, you are aware that some areas of your life are well developed. Welcome to the club. I have never known anyone who is a great role model in everything. All you have to do is model what you are good at, and then model growth in your areas of deficiency.

The major role model in my life is Jim Conway. He is an outstanding communicator and probably the most vulnerable man I know. He shares his struggles and victories with equal skill. He is gifted at helping men recover from bad decisions or painful backgrounds. I have learned much from him about how to engage in ministry that reaches the hearts of people. This is what he is best at.

When it comes to raising sons, however, I never expected him to speak from experience because he raised all daughters. He didn't have wrestling contests in his living room. He didn't ask the question every time he bought something, "How long will this last until my boys break it?" He didn't deal with the burping contests that took place in my home whenever the coast was clear. I respected his opinions about raising boys, but I never expected him to speak from experience.

If you are good at auto mechanics, pass it on. If you are good at hunting, pass it on. If you are good at studying the Bible, pass it on. If you are good at computers, pass it on. Whatever you are good at, pass it on. You don't have to be something that you aren't. You just need to be good at what you are good at. Those who are watching will be better because you did what you were best at.

Be an Encourager

I believe Hebrews 3:13 is one of the most strategic verses in the Bible when it comes to influencing others. It says, "Encourage one another daily, as long as it is called Today, so that none of you may be hardened by sin's deceitfulness." The need for encouragement exists because sin is trying to deceive all of us and harden our hearts. When we talk about encouraging, we are not talking about just being nice to each other so we all feel better. We are talking about winning the war for the hearts of those we love.

The word for *encourage* is the Greek word *parakaleo*. It is made up of two words, *para*, which means "alongside," and *kaleo*, which means "call." To encourage someone, therefore, is to be called alongside another person to bring out the best in him or her. It is a tough word that involves a commitment of time, money, energy, and affirmation. It is the dedication to do whatever it takes to help this person be his best.

Paul models what it means to encourage in 1 Thessalonians 2:10-12. He told the believers in Thessalonica he was doing his best when he said, "You are witness, and so is God, of how holy, righteous and blameless we were among you who believed." We know from the context that Paul is pointing to the fact that he worked hard so he wouldn't be a burden to them. He did his best so they could focus on their own growth. Then he said that he encouraged, comforted, and urged them on just "as a father deals with his own children" (v. 11). He worked hard among them. He cheered them on. He urged them to be their best. He looked for ways to help them advance. You can tell from these words that he didn't always know what to do. He just kept looking for ways to help them until he found what was working. That is encouragement.

John Wooden pointed out the need for encouragement when he said, "Young people need models, not critics."[5] The late Jim Valvano, college basketball coach and founder of the V Foundation for Cancer Research, pointed out the power of encouragement when he said, "My father gave me the greatest gift anyone could give another person, he believed in me."[6]

The heart of encouragement is focusing on the other person. You cannot force people to be like you, nor should you want to, but you can profoundly help people be themselves.

Geoffrey de Havilland, the British aviation pioneer and aircraft engineer, learned this one day as he took his sons flying. He was hoping to instill in them his passion for flying, but it turned out his sons had different passions. His three-year-old son wanted to know which way his spit would blow, while his five-year-old, who was crazy about trains, asked if they could follow the railway lines he could see below.[7] Geoffrey helped his sons develop their pursuits, but those pursuits were much different from dad's.

Say, "I Am Sorry"

No matter how hard you work at being a good role model, you will make mistakes. You will say things that you regret. You will do things you wish you could take back. You will miss opportunities to grow that will cause suffering in the lives of those you love. This is the plight of all men. If you somehow managed to be perfect, we would crucify you, so I'm not sure you want that to be your goal. When you are aware that you have fallen short and legitimately disappointed the people who are watching, apologize.

Specifically admit what you have done. If you become aware of something you have done that you wouldn't want others to emulate, admit it.

I once worked in the oil fields in Bakersfield, California, and as you might imagine, it was a pretty rough place with some crude individuals. I asked God to help me be a good role model so that maybe somebody's life would be affected. I got put on a crew with an inquisitive young man, and I figured this was my opportunity. We started talking every day about life and our futures. One day he asked me, "Do you ever swear?"

"Actually, I don't," I said. "Knowing Jesus is important to me, and my wife doesn't like swearing, so I've been working on it. I'm not sure why it's not a big struggle for me, but it isn't."

Wouldn't you know it, two days later I swore. It just blurted out. Compared to the way the other men talked, what I said was mild. But I had gone on record, and somebody was watching. I asked Jesus to use my apology, and at lunchtime I admitted my slip to my new friend and apologized. He said it wasn't necessary, but I knew it was.

When you apologize, avoid making statements such as, "I can tell you are upset, so if there's anything I have done that hurt your feelings, I am sorry." This isn't actually an apology. It's a statement about the other person's reaction rather than you owning up to your actions. It's the same as saying, "I'm sorry you have thin skin and that you got hurt when you shouldn't have. I guess I'll have to apologize because you are too weak to handle real life." If you want to confront someone for overreacting, then confront. Don't disguise your confrontation as an apology.

So what does an apology sound like then?

Find a way to express regret. Those who are watching will be asking, "Does he mean it?" They will primarily take into account your tone of voice and body language to decide if you truly are sorry or if you trying to manipulate them.

The tone of voice that demonstrates you are sorry is softer than your normal tone of voice. If you have a coach's voice, you'll want to leave that out of this conversation. Loud voices communicate authority and power. Strong voices are employed when you want people to get things done. When you are apologizing, you will want to choose a softer tone that says, "I am aware of what I have done, and I wish I had done differently." Be sincere and don't plead. You want to model that mistakes are a part of life. They don't ruin your influence and they don't disqualify instantly.

Body language that matches an apology is likewise gentler than your normal body language. To create gentle body language, try these suggestions:

- Get on the same eye level as the other person.

- Look them in the eyes and relax the muscles around your eyes.

- When you break eye contact, look down.

- Lean a little bit forward. If you lean back, you appear defensive. If you lean too far forward, you appear intimidating.

Ask, "Will you forgive me?" Since you are apologizing in the context of a being a role model, it's a two-way relationship. You don't want to end the conversation until there is some response from the other person. If you receive forgiveness, your influence kicks back into gear and respect grows. If forgiveness is withheld, you will still be influential, but the other person will struggle to keep his or her heart soft, and growth will be harder.

It's best, therefore, for the other person to offer forgiveness. Don't rush this. Forgiveness doesn't have to be instantaneous, although it's awesome when it happens that way. Feel free to give the other person a day or a week to work through the process. You just want to make sure you make forgiveness part of the conversation so you model what it takes to keep your heart open.

Laugh and Have Fun

Golfer Phil Mickelson was once asked whether his dad was like Tiger Woods's father, Earl, who had Tiger playing golf at the age of two. Mickelson said, "No, my dad was fun."[8]

Life is serious, but it works best when it's balanced with fun memories and times of laughter. Even the Bible says, "A cheerful heart is good medicine" (Proverbs 17:22). God knows that we need to enjoy the journey, so He designed us to be attracted to people who laugh and make us laugh.

I actually think you have to work at not laughing because life is funny. For instance, there was a lady in our church who stood out from the rest. She would usually show up in clothes that didn't match. On the Fourth of July weekend, she came dressed in a black and gold outfit with a red, white, and blue vest. She had a habit of checking in with me every Sunday to give me a report of the most outrageous thing that happened that week.

One day she came up to me and said, "Bill, I went to the doctor this week. He told me I have arthritis. I have bursitis. And I have ridiculitis."

My first thought was, *I knew there was a name for this.* I meant to keep my mouth shut, but instead I said, "Eleanor, I could have saved you $35." Fortunately we had a good relationship, so we both laughed, I prayed for her, and we got on with the week.

My good friend Dan is a gifted engineer who is always looking for ways to improve life. His family loved camping, so they connected with two other families who loved camping. Year after year they spent their summer vacations together. He got to thinking, "We don't have hot water and there are a lot of us. I bet I can do something about this."

When he pulled into the camping site the next year, he had a hot-water heater mounted on the roof of his station wagon. He routed water lines, complete with a recirculation pump, from the heater into the engine compartment and around the engine. As long as the engine was running, the water would get hotter. He looked ridiculous, but he arrived with 40 gallons of hot water for his friends and family to enjoy.

I could go on. If you keep your eyes and ears open, you will find that life is filled with humor. When you stay in tune with it and retell the stories, people are drawn to you. When you save jokes and share them, people are drawn to you. When you laugh at the unexpected turns in life rather than exploding in anger, people are drawn to you. The good news is you can cultivate a sense of humor.

Look for jokes and stories. The Internet is filled with information that will make you laugh. Books are filled with stories and anecdotes that make people smile. Most sermons or public presentations contain humor that is worthy to be shared. Almost all movies have humorous moments in them that make for great conversation starters. As you collect these and tell them to the people you rub shoulders with, good relationships develop.

Write down the funny things you hear. When my oldest son was playing football in college, a young man on the team had a knack for saying things you never forget. He approached his coach one day and said, "Coach, do you know why I give 100 percent at every practice? Do you know why I try my absolute hardest every time I get on the field?"

His coach told me that he was pleased at first. He thought, *Maybe I'm getting through to these guys. It seems like they're getting it when it comes to teamwork and the value of their effort.* In anticipation he said, "I think so, but tell me what's on your mind."

"Well, it's like this, coach. I know that for most of these young men, this might be the last time they see greatness, and I don't want them to miss their chance."

I recently attended a Fellowship of Christian Athletes event that coincided with the Holiday Bowl. Afterward, I was talking with a couple on FCA staff who are good friends, and I asked them, "How are you two doing?"

"We're doing good," they said. "In fact, real good. We're trying to figure out the whole multiplying thing, and we think we might have succeeded." They didn't say they might be pregnant. They didn't say they were hoping to get pregnant. They were trying to "figure out the multiplying thing."

Practice laughing out loud. You will surely have some funny experiences in the next few days. You may see a funny movie, hear a funny story, or listen to a comedian. When you do, laugh out loud. Don't hold back. Don't worry about what other people think. Don't suppress the response. Just enjoy the moment and laugh.

Share Your Story

Since being a role model is based on accepting that people are watching, you will be most effective when you actively share your story. You can do this in words by sharing what you know, and you can do this with actions by getting involved in people's lives. Often, your biggest moments happen when you are active and say little.

Your life is having an impact, and you can maximize your influence if you look for ways to pass on what you are best at. Here are a few skills you can work on that will help you accomplish this.

Listen to your best advice, then repeat it often. If you pay attention, you'll notice there are a few pieces of really good advice you give regularly. These are statements you have said so often, you may not realize how important they are. If you can identify them and then deliberately repeat them, you can focus your influence. Some of the statements I have homed in on are:

- Have a short memory when it comes to your mistakes.
- Don't just talk about it, be about it.
- Game on.
- Man up.

- Boundaries are decisions you make to maintain self-respect.

- Experience is what you get when you don't get what you want.

- Life is a competitive sport.

- You can do everything God has called you to do.

- Give your *A* priorities *A* effort.

- God always gets His will done. We can get there the easy way or we can get there the hard way, but we will get there. (Just ask Jonah.)

- Routine things should have a system. Creative things should have freedom.

I look for opportunities to repeat these sayings because I believe they are true and they motivate me to action. I figure the people who are listening will eventually get them if I say them enough times in enough different settings.

For Christmas this year, my youngest son, Caleb, shared an essay he wrote for a college class. He gave me credit as a mentor in his life, and one of the things he emphasized was the need to have a short memory so you don't focus too hard on your mistakes. Mission accomplished.

Invite others to join you in projects. There are certain pursuits and projects that you are good at. You are confident when you do these because of your skill level. You can extend your influence if you invite others to help you with these projects. At first, they may slow you down a little, but in the long run, you will extend your influence and enhance the lives of people you care about.

I mentioned that I have remodeled every house I have owned. Since I enjoy this and seem to be able to figure out these projects, I have intentionally invited my sons to get involved. A note of caution: My sons did not share my passion for my home-remodel projects when they were young. It was my house, not theirs. It was my idea, not theirs. It would have been easy for me to be critical and pushy with them to the point they hated the project. I had to give them assignments they could do and find some fulfillment in. I wasn't sure if they would ever really enjoy remodeling, but I wanted them to be exposed to something I enjoyed and knew they would benefit from as adults.

My plan began to pay off last summer. My oldest son owns a home that has a daylight basement. During the rainy season, the carpet in the basement is perpetually wet. He attempted to figure out the problem, but got stuck. So he asked if I could spend a few days with him to see if we could problem-solve together.

It was a remarkably satisfying time for me. The problem was a ground-level window that wasn't sealed properly. Water was running down the hill and under the window. Brock listened attentively as I demonstrated how to build a retaining wall to create more clearance for the window. Then together we figured out how to seal the window and rebuild the windowsill. For the first time, one of my sons outworked me. Late on the second afternoon, I sat on the retaining wall we had built and watched my son work for an hour. It was awesome to switch roles for a while.

Spend time with people. Since we all become like the people we spend time with, you can be an effective role model if you have a plan for spending time with people who are important to you. You can do this informally and formally.

Informally, you can include people in your social life. Sharing meals together, vacationing together, and attending social functions all add to our relationships. During these informal gatherings, stories are told, problems are naturally solved, and skills are caught.

Formally, you can make commitments to be involved in people's lives. You can join an athletic league, community theatre, singing group, or hunting club. You can get involved in your local church. You can join a Bible study or small group where you talk about principles and how to apply them to your life.

You can read books with a group. If you've enjoyed this book, you may consider forming a small group to read the book together and discuss with each other the action steps you intend to pursue. (Discussion questions are available to assist your group at www.billandpam.org.) As you discuss what you are reading, you get a much deeper grasp of the truths contained in it. You can do this with any book you read and extend the impact into your life and the lives of those who are important to you.

The bottom line is that your life counts. You are opening a door that can never be closed. You are making a difference in the lives of others. Decide to make it happen.

Just for Fun

Harry Neidig points out the funny things that can happen when you sign up to be a role model:

> On the way back from a Cub Scouts meeting, my grandson asked my son the question. "Dad, I know that babies come from mommies' tummies, but how do they get there in the first place?" he asked innocently.
>
> After my son hemmed and hawed for a while, my grandson finally spoke up in disgust. "You don't have to make something up, Dad. It's okay if you don't know the answer."[9]

Notes

Introduction

1. Jeffrey Kluger, "Rocket Scientist Robert Goddard," *Time*, March 29, 1999, www.time.com/time/magazine/article/0,9171,990613-2,00.html#ixzz0bNe1zEmZ

Chapter 1: Decide to Be Decisive

1. Mike Penner, "99 Things about John Wooden," *Los Angeles Times*, October 14, 2009, http://articles.latimes.com/2009/oct/14/sports/sp-john-wooden14?pg=2
2. www.quoteland.com/author.asp?AUTHOR_ID=532
3. http://www.quotes.net/quote/6382
4. www.answers.com/topic/william-a-foster
5. "The bath and the bucket story," www.businessballs.com/stories.htm#the-two-bulls-story
6. www.businessballs.com/stories.htm#the-blind-golfers-story

Chapter 2: Decide to Seek an Adventure

1. http://quotations.about.com/cs/inspirationquotes/a/Courage1.htm
2. Information found at the Jewish Virtual Library, a division of the American-Israeli Cooperative Enterprise. www.jewishvirtuallibrary.org/jsource/biography/abraham.html
3. http://everything2.com/title/President+George+W.+Bush+to+the+300th+graduating+class+of+Yale+University

Chapter 3: Decide to Be Competitive

1. www.surfersam.com/friends/football2.htm
2. www.ultimate-youth-basketball-guide.com/coach-k-quotes.html
3. www.wow4u.com/helloquotesfrom/index.html
4. http://quotations.about.com/cs/inspirationquotes/a/OvercomingAd1.htm
5. http://quotations.about.com/cs/inspirationquotes/a/Confidence1.htm
6. Ibid.
7. Ibid.
8. www.wow4u.com/helloquotesfrom/index.html
9. www.ultimate-youth-basketball-guide.com/coach-k-quotes.html
10. www.ultimate-youth-basketball-guide.com/john-wooden-quotes.html

11. www.surfersam.com/friends/football2.htm

12. www.mylifecoach.com/inspirationalquotes.htm

13. www.anecdotage.com/index.php?aid=4677

14. http://blog.guykawasaki.com/2006/04/six_more_crazy_.html#ixzz0bPjcgJTM

Chapter 4: Decide to Set Goals

1. http://thinkexist.com/search/searchquotation.asp?search=goal+setting

2. www.danieljanssen.com/wordpictures/buildwisecarpenter.shtml

3. www.famous-quotes.com/author.php?aid=4893

4. http://dictionary.reference.com/browse/mentor

5. www.timesonline.co.uk/tol/sport/columnists/rod_liddle/article6945794.ece

6. www.motivational-inspirational-corner.com/getquote.html?categoryid=19

7. www.mylifecoach.com/inspirationalquotes.htm

8. www.kidsgoals.com/kids-jokes.shtml

Chapter 5: Decide to Be Busy

1. www.inspirationalspark.com/overcoming-fear-quotes-quotations.html

2. www.sundtmemorial.org/site/c.eeIGLNOrGnF/b.3041213/

3. www.ahajokes.com/farm011.html

Chapter 6: Decide to Be Better

1. http://articles.latimes.com/2009/oct/14/sports/sp-john-wooden14

2. http://sannyasin.com/jokes.html

3. www.bolthouse.com/html/cs_comp_overviewn.html

4. www.thebolthousefoundation.org

5. www.focusonthefamily.com/socialissues/pornography/pornography.aspx

6. Fritz Rienecker and Cleon Rogers, *Linguistic Key to the Greek New Testament* (Grand Rapids, MI: Zondervan Publishing House, 1980), 769.

7. Ibid.

8. www.skywriting.net/inspirational/humor/pilots—on_the_radio.html

Chapter 7: Decide to Love

1. www.ultimate-youth-basketball-guide.com/coaching-quotes.html

2. www.rd.com/clean-jokes-and-laughs/our-50-funniest-true-stories/article93740-1.html

3. Temperament websites include: https://timlahaye.com/shopexd.asp?id=147; www.oneishy.com/personality/personality_test.php; http://classervices.com/shopsite_sc/store/html/page1.html; www.ministryinsights.com/parable/; http://us.personalstrengths.com/sdi.php?id=100

4. www.anecdotage.com/index.php?aid=635

Chapter 8: Decide to Be a Friend of God

1. www.goodreads.com/author/quotes/46261.Muhammad_Ali
2. www.care2.com/c2c/groups/disc.html?gpp=2892&pst=935110

Chapter 9: Decide to Be a Man of Principle

1. www.ultimate-youth-basketball-guide.com/coach-k-quotes.html
2. Ray Kennedy, "Good Man in the Long Run," *Sports Illustrated*, September 8, 1975 (http://sports illustrated.cnn.com/vault/article/magazine/MAG1090211/5/index.htm).
3. www.dispatch.com/live/content/sports/stories/2009/09/04/0_ARCHIE_GRIFFIN.ART_ART_09-04-09_A1_F9EVFH7.html
4. www.youmeworks.com/sometimesyoushouldntlisten.html
5. www.wow4u.com/helloquotesfrom/index.html
6. www.divorcerate.org
7. Mike Penner, "99 Things about John Wooden," *Los Angeles Times*, October 14, 2009 (http://articles.latimes.com/2009/oct/14/sports/sp-john-wooden14?pg=3).
8. www.surfersam.com/friends/football2.htm
9. www.duncanentertainment.com/interview_griffin.php
10. www.rd.com/clean-jokes-and-laughs/our-50-funniest-true-stories/article93740-2.html

Chapter 10: Decide to Be a Role Model

1. www.famousquotesandauthors.com/topics/role_models_quotes.html
2. www.anecdotage.com/index.php?aid=3549
3. www.anecdotage.com/index.php?aid=15534
4. www.anecdotage.com/index.php?aid=11340
5. www.coachlikeapro.com/john-wooden.html
6. www.wow4u.com/helloquotesfrom/index.html
7. www.anecdotage.com/index.php?aid=1678
8. www.anecdotage.com/index.php?aid=7682
9. www.rd.com/clean-jokes-and-laughs/our-50-funniest-true-stories/article93740-1.html

■ ■ ■

For more resources to enhance your relationships
and build marriages or to connect with Bill and Pam Farrel
for a speaking engagement, contact

Farrel Communications
Masterful Living Ministries
3755 Avocado Boulevard, #414
La Mesa, CA 91941

800-810-4449

info@billandpam.org

www.billandpam.org

For discussion questions and further study, visit
www.billandpam.org/men

■ ■ ■

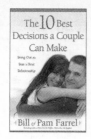

The 10 Best Decisions a Couple Can Make: Bring Out the Best in Your Relationship
BILL FARREL AND PAM FARREL

Bill and Pam Farrel, bestselling authors of *Men Are Like Waffles— Women Are Like Spaghetti*, lead husbands and wives through the ten most influential decisions a couple can make to shape a lasting and loving marriage.

Exploring romance, communication, sex, conflict resolution, family, and personalities, the Farrels walk couples through the ten decisions that will

- turn me and me into "we"
- redeem past bad choices and give hope for a solid future
- bring balance to roller coaster emotions
- create a life together of trust, grace, and understanding

Filled with practical advice, biblical insights, and the Farrels' trademark warmth and wit, this manual is a terrific gift for newlyweds and just as valuable for long-time marriage partners.

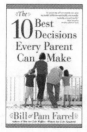

The 10 Best Decisions Every Parent Can Make
BILL FARREL AND PAM FARREL

Bill and Pam Farrel are the parents of three active children. From their personal experience comes wisdom and encouragement for other parents. The Farrels offer ideas for loving and nurturing special needs, strong-willed, and prodigal children.

With real-life examples and biblical inspiration, this book examines the 10 best decisions parents can make to unlock the unique gifts inside their children, including

- temperament
- goals
- talents
- spiritual development
- leadership abilities

Packed with creative, motivational tools and games that allow children to blossom and succeed, this resource is a great gift or tool for parents who want their children to become everything God designed them to be.

The 10 Best Decisions a Woman Can Make:
Finding Your Place in God's Plan
PAM FARREL

Women today have important decisions to make about family, career, and ministry. Sometimes the daily choices seem overwhelming. Popular author and speaker Pam Farrel encourages women to discover the joy of finding their place in God's plan as they

- stop pleasing people and start pleasing God
- find a positive place to direct their creativity, energy, and enthusiasm
- gain confidence about the value of their time and efforts
- assess their strengths and weaknesses, skills, and talents

Pam's motivating, liberating message will empower women to pursue God's best for their life.

This popular book, now with a fresh new cover for today's readers, includes a study guide and discussion questions for personal or small group use.

To learn more about other Harvest House books
or to read sample chapters, log on to our website:

www.harvesthousepublishers.com

HARVEST HOUSE PUBLISHERS

EUGENE, OREGON

ALSO BY
KATHERINE E. KREUTER

Fool Me Once
The Cloud Nine Affair